Hot Links

HOT LINKS

Literature Links for the Middle School Curriculum

Cora M. Wright

Marilyn Wright, Illustrator

1998
LIBRARIES UNLIMITED, INC.
and Its Division
Teacher Ideas Press
Englewood, Colorado

Many thanks to my husband, Tom,
who shares my love of literature
and gave advice
and technical direction.
A lifetime of thanks goes to my parents,
who shared their love of reading with me.

LIBRARIES UNLIMITED, INC.
and Its Division
Teacher Ideas Press
P.O. Box 6633
Englewood, CO 80155-6633
1-800-237-6124
www.lu.com

Production Editor: Kay Mariea
Copy Editor: Thea De Hart
Proofreader: Susie Sigman
Design and Layout: Pamela J. Getchell

Library of Congress Cataloging-in-Publication Data

Wright, Cora M.
    Hot links : literature links for the middle school curriculum /
Cora M. Wright ; Marilyn Wright, illustrator.
    ix, 173 p. 17x25 cm.
    Includes bibliographical references and index.
    ISBN 1-56308-587-9 (softbound)
    1. Children's literature--Bibliography.   2. Middle school
students--United States--Books and reading.   I. Title.
Z1037.W955   1998
011.62--dc21   98-36039
                                                            CIP

CONTENTS

ACKNOWLEDGMENTS

Technical assistance was given by Tom Wright, who patiently waded through this project and learned lots in the process. Thanks again.

A book is so much more fun when it has illustrations, and we have Marilyn Wright to thank for her original drawings of Willy the Worm, who winds his way through our book.

INTRODUCTION

The world of children's literature is an exciting place with outstanding works published in the past and hundreds of marvelous new books being produced every year. The quality of writing and illustrating continues to change and improve, making the creation of children's literature a true art form. With so many high-quality books from which to choose, book selection by librarians, teachers, parents, and students may become difficult. The goal of this book is to guide the user in book selection for recreational reading and in connection with all curriculum areas. I have chosen both newly published and older, "tried and true" titles on the basis of their quality of writing, how well the illustrations accompany the text, the interest to students, availability, and a strong curriculum connection.

Many of the books included in this collection are multifaceted, allowing them to fit into more than one category or curriculum. The annotation is included in the section considered most appropriate for each book, but if it fits into another category, a brief summary is included in that additional category, along with a note at the end referencing the section that includes the annotation. A table at the back of this book, arranged alphabetically by title, indicates the curriculum connections for each book.

If you'd like to correspond with me, please e-mail me at towright@ pacbell.net.

Happy reading!

Chapter 1

BIOGRAPHIES

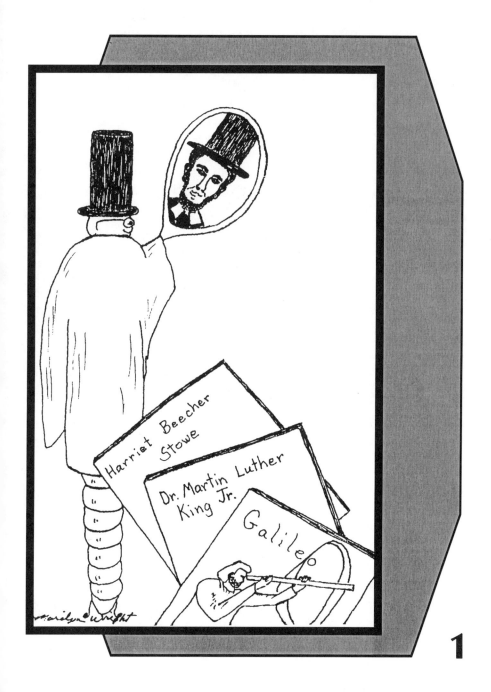

Wonderfully written, attractive, and informative biographies are plentiful in the children's literature world at this time, and students love to read the "real" stories. The books in this section were selected because of their close connection with other curricula, making them useful with specific topics or enjoyable as recreational reading to help readers discover inspiring, interesting people.

Bray, Rosemary. **Martin Luther King**. Illus. Malcah Zeldis. New York: Greenwillow, 1995. 48p. $16.00. ISBN 0-688-13131-X.
　　Colorful folk-art paintings along with informative extended text make this an excellent biography of Martin Luther King Jr. The King family was a middle-class Black family with a comfortable lifestyle, but the segregation laws in Atlanta, Georgia, affected them just as much as other Blacks. This book explains and describes Martin's strong feelings about these inequities, his thirst for knowledge, his search for justice, and how childhood shaped his life's work. The picture-book format makes the book inviting, and the extended text provides a great deal of frank, open information. His work and the reasons behind his actions are described in text that begs to be read aloud.

Cooney, Miriam P. **Celebrating Women in Mathematics and Science**. Short biographies of important women. *See* MATHEMATICS.

Cumpián, Carlos. **Latino Rainbow: Poems About Latino Americans**. Biographies about important Latino Americans written in poem form. *See* MULTICULTURAL.

Everett, Gwen. **John Brown: One Man Against Slavery**. Illus. Jacob Lawrence. New York: Rizzoli Children's Library, 1993. 32p. $16.00. ISBN 0-8478-1702-4.
　　John Brown, a free Black man, was convinced that one man could make a difference. It was his dream to free every Black slave. Ignoring other abolitionists—such as Frederick Douglass, who advocated peaceful methods—he mounted military attacks on plantations to free the slaves. He believed he and other volunteers needed to go from plantation to plantation, attacking the owners, freeing slaves as they went. His violent raids lasted only a short time before he was captured and hung. John Brown's story is told from the perspective of his daughter, who is

convinced that even though his crusade was short-lived, it was an important event leading to the Civil War. The paintings by Jacob Lawrence are bold, descriptive, and informative.

Fritz, Jean. **Harriet Beecher Stowe and the Beecher Preachers**. New York: G. P. Putnam's Sons, 1994. 144p. $15.95. ISBN 0-399-22666-4.

When President Lincoln met Harriet Beecher Stowe, he called her the "little lady who made this big war." She never intended to be responsible for the Civil War, but she did intend to do something about the slavery issue. Harriet grew up in a family strongly controlled by her father, Lyman Beecher, a famous fire and brimstone preacher in the 1800s. Because she was a girl, she couldn't become one of "his preachers," his term for his six sons; at that time women were not allowed to speak in public and were expected to be loyal and faithful wives and mothers. This was difficult for Harriet, an opinionated, bright, creative person, who needed to make her thoughts known. She did indeed marry and have a family, but her real love was writing and drawing. Taking care of six children left little time for these passions, but she squeezed them in and helped support the family by selling short stories to magazines. She wrote *Uncle Tom's Cabin* to "do something" about slavery; it first appeared as a serial in a magazine. She became an instant success, and her fame spread throughout the world, especially England.

This biography helps students to understand why Harriet wrote what she did, the attitudes about slavery before the Civil War, and the status of women at this time. This book is well researched and includes many black-and-white photographs of Beecher family members and places where they lived and traveled. Fritz's writing pieces the family's story together into an interesting, readable, entertaining biography. An extensive bibliography and index are included. This work fits well when studying the Civil War or the women's rights movement.

Glass, Andrew. **The Sweetwater Run: The Story of Buffalo Bill Cody and the Pony Express**. The story of the Pony Express is told through the eyes of Buffalo Bill Cody. *See* SOCIAL STUDIES—UNITED STATES HISTORY.

Krull, Kathleen. **Lives of the Artists: Masterpieces, Messes (and What the Neighbors Thought)**. Biographies of famous artists. *See* FINE ARTS.

———. **Lives of the Athletes: Thrills, Spills (and What the Neighbors Thought)**. Biographies of twenty athletes. *See* SPORTS AND GAMES.

———. **Lives of the Musicians: Good Times, Bad Times (and What the Neighbors Thought)**. Biographies of famous musicians. *See* FINE ARTS.

————. **Lives of the Writers: Comedies, Tragedies (and What the Neighbors Thought)**. Illus. Kathryn Hewitt. New York: Harcourt Brace & Company, 1994. 96p. $18.95. ISBN 0-15-248009-9.

> The 19 authors presented in this collection represent different countries, time periods, and literary forms and styles, but they all were persistent, which led to success, and all are still widely read today. Each writer is illustrated in a full-page picture done in a slightly cartoonlike style with an oversized head clothed in representative costume. Three pages of text give an interesting biography of the writer, often pointing out unique and funny characteristics or anecdotes, which make the writer real to the reader. At the end of each article a footnote entitled "Bookmarks" gives additional, interesting tidbits about the person and his or her work. The entries include Murasaki Shikibu, Miguel de Cervantes, Jane Austen, Hans Christian Andersen, Edgar Allan Poe, Charles Dickens, Charlotte and Emily Brontë, Emily Dickinson, Louisa May Alcott, Mark Twain, Frances Hodgson Burnett, Robert Louis Stevenson, Jack London, Carl Sandburg, E. B. White, Zora Neale Hurston, Langston Hughes, and Isaac Bashevis Singer. This is an outstanding collection—well written, informative, and entertaining. A list of literary terms, an index, and a bibliography are included.

Lasky, Kathryn. **The Librarian Who Measured the Earth**. The biography of Eratosthenes, the Greek scientist, mathematician, author, and geographer, is told in a delightful and informative manner. *See* MATHEMATICS.

McCully, Emily Arnold. **The Ballot Box Battle**. New York: Alfred A. Knopf, 1996. $17.00. ISBN 0-679-97938-7.

> Women's right to vote is taken for granted today, but this simple book clearly points out that the struggle to gain that right was hard and long. Lizzie Stanton is presented through the eyes of a young girl, Cordelia, who is frustrated that she can't please her father because she is a girl rather than a boy. Cordelia's observations of Lizzie Stanton's struggle for women's suffrage teaches her to be courageous and strong. Although Cordelia is shown as a young girl, the subject matter is for older readers interested in women's rights. The author's notes give additional information about Lizzie Stanton and her fight for women's rights.

Nichol, Barbara. **Beethoven Lives Upstairs**. Illus. Scott Cameron. This biography of Ludwig van Beethoven is told through letters between a boy and his uncle. *See* UNIQUE PRESENTATIONS.

Parker, Nancy Winslow. **Locks, Crocs, & Skeeters**. The story of the Panama Canal is told through the biographies of people important to the canal. *See* UNIQUE PRESENTATIONS.

Reimer, Luetta, and Wilbert Reimer. **Mathematicians Are People, Too: Stories from the Lives of Great Mathematicians**. Fifteen biographies of famous mathematicians are written in an easy-to-understand manner designed to spark interest in mathematics. *See* MATHEMATICS.

Schroeder, Alan. **Minty: A Story of Young Harriet Tubman**. Illus. Jerry Pinkney. New York: Dial Books for Young Readers, 1996. Unpaged. $16.99. ISBN 0-8037-1888-8 (trade), 0-8037-1889-6 (lib bdg.).

> After reading this book, it's easier to understand why Harriet Tubman was able to accomplish so much. As a young slave, she was constantly testing and questioning, even though it cost her dearly at times. She was known as a "difficult" slave and was punished often, despite family members' admonishment that she conform. Harriet was committed to doing what was right, to finding some justice in an unjust society, and if possible, to making changes. These are the qualities that enabled her to do great and heroic deeds through the Underground Railroad during her adult life. The illustrations by Pinkney are bold and descriptive and augment the text.

Sis, Peter. **Starry Messenger: A Book Depicting the Life of a Famous Scientist, Mathematician, Astronomer, Philosopher, Physicist, Galileo Galilei**. An exciting, descriptive, and uniquely presented biography of Galileo. *See* SCIENCE.

Spivak, Dawnine. **Grass Sandals: The Travels of Basho**. Illus. Demi. A biography of the seventeenth-century Japanese poet. *See* POETRY.

Stanley, Diane. **Leonardo da Vinci**. New York: Morrow Junior Books, 1996. 48p. $16.00. ISBN 0-688-10437-1 (trade), 0-688-10438-X (lib. bdg.).

> Although we look upon Leonardo da Vinci as one of the world's most outstanding artists and a pioneer of modern invention, Diane Stanley points out that his life was rather tragic. He was the son of an important man, but his mother's peasant background caused him to be shunned by his wealthy family. Leonardo was a genius but had trouble concentrating on any one thing, so he led a lonely, sad life, wandering from city to city, with few people truly appreciating him during his lifetime. Toward the end of his life Leonardo was befriended by the king of France, Francis I, who appreciated his work and made life more comfortable for him. Although he was a prolific artist and writer, most of his work was lost. We are fortunate to have the dozen known paintings. His copious notes regarding scientific research and inventions were forgotten for centuries, and only a portion was recovered in the 1800s. The illustrations and sketches by Stanley vividly depict da Vinci's life, and a pronunciation guide, a postscript, and an extensive bibliography make this a useful and informative book.

Stanley, Diane, and Peter Vennema. **Good Queen Bess: The Story of Elizabeth I of England**. New York: Four Winds Press, 1990. 40p. $17.00. ISBN 0-02-786810-9.

      Henry VIII's greatest fear was that he would have no son to inherit the throne. This fear became a reality when his only son, Edward, died six years after becoming king, leaving the succession to the throne in shambles. After Bloody Mary's death in 1558, her half sister, Elizabeth, became queen at age 25. Elizabeth was well educated, wise, and able to speak several languages. She was a skilled negotiator, able to appease leaders from other countries as well as maintain peace in her own land. She ruled wisely for 45 years, earning the name Good Queen Bess. She never married and left no heirs. The well-told story acquaints the reader with a great woman and the history of her time.

Chapter 2

ENGLISH—CLASSICS

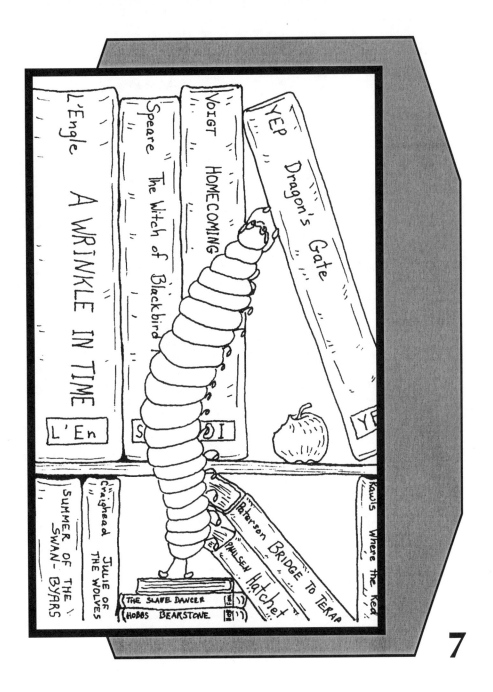

Some books are simply "must reads" and should be encountered somewhere in a reader's reading career. The titles included in this section are not the "classics" such as *Moby Dick* or *Gulliver's Travels* but are books published within the last 40 years that have stood the test of time and consistently delight readers. Many of these titles make excellent core literature books to read and study as an entire class or in small groups.

Avi. **The True Confessions of Charlotte Doyle**. New York: Orchard, 1990. $14.95. ISBN 0-531-05893-X (trade), 0-531-08493-0 (lib. bdg.), 0-380-71475-2pa.

When the Doyle family is summoned back to the United States in 1832, Charlotte is allowed to finish the school year in Liverpool, England, with the promise that she'll voyage on the ship *Seahawk* in June along with another family. She arrives at the docks only to discover that the family will not be making the voyage and that she is the only female aboard the ship bound for Providence, Rhode Island. To compound the problem, the sailors are about to mutiny against the tyrannical Captain Jaggery. An impetuous teenager, Charlotte makes decisions too quickly and speaks up when she shouldn't, putting herself in severe danger both from the sailors and the captain. Every time she turns around Charlotte finds herself in another dangerous situation, including working as a crewmember climbing the rigging. The description of this climb is classic, and readers' hands will become shaky and sweaty while reading this episode. This novel, filled with mystery and intrigue, portrays a strong female main character and includes marvelous descriptions of sailing in the 1800s. The Appendix includes sketches of the ship with labels for each main part. Ship's time is also explained. Life at this time is well portrayed—especially women's place in society—and the surprise ending adds a perfect touch to an exciting book.

Byars, Betsy. **The Summer of the Swans**. Illus. Ted CoConis. New York: Viking, 1970. 142p. $13.50. ISBN 0-670-68190-3, 0-380-00098-9pa.

Sara has always taken good care of her retarded brother, Charlie, but now that she's becoming a teenager and is concerned about how she looks, what she's wearing, and the opinions of those around her, Charlie is getting in the way. Once a year swans land in a pond outside the town, and although Charlie can't speak, he makes it clear to Sara that he wants to see the swans. She reluctantly takes him there but only for a brief time because she has other plans. During the night Charlie decides to try to find the swans by himself but becomes hopelessly lost and confused. He's neither able to call for help nor to answer when searchers look for him. Sara is distraught and blames herself for Charlie's disappearance. The entire town joins in the search and finds him, and Sara discovers that even those people she thought were making fun of Charlie really do care about him. This is an important work that all students should be encouraged to read at some time because it says so much about accepting ourselves and those who are not like us. Betsy Byars deservedly earned the Newbery Medal for this book.

Christopher, John. **The City of Gold and Lead**. The second book in the White Mountains trilogy. Will and Fritz get inside the City of the Tripods and attempt to find out how the system works. *See* READ ALOUDS.

————. **The Pool of Fire**. The final book in the White Mountains trilogy. Will and Fritz's aim is to attack the Tripods and overthrow them. *See* READ ALOUDS.

————. **The White Mountains**. In this first book in the White Mountains trilogy the decision is made to flee to the White Mountains to escape the control of the Tripods. *See* READ ALOUDS.

Collier, James Lincoln, and Christopher Collier. **My Brother Sam Is Dead**. This is an historically accurate account of the Revolutionary War as seen through the eyes of 13-year-old Tim Meeker. *See* SOCIAL STUDIES—UNITED STATES HISTORY.

Cooper, Susan. **The Dark Is Rising**. New York: Atheneum, 1973. 216p. $13.50. ISBN 0-689-30317-3, 0-590-43319-9pa.
Will Stanton is an ordinary kid growing up in the countryside of England when he is visited by the Old Ones, who need him to help in the battle between the Dark and the Light. He is taken back in time to engage in the quest to win against the Dark, which is often dangerous, filled with the unknown, and frightening. In the world of fantasy, the struggle between good and evil is often the main theme, but The Dark Is Rising series rises above all others in this quest. The other books in the series are *Over Sea/Under Stone, Greenwitch, The Grey King*, and *Silver on the Tree*. This is a classic series that will be enjoyed by fantasy fans. Both *The Grey King* and *The Dark Is Rising* were Newbery Award recipients.

Fox, Paula. **The Slave Dancer**. The story of the slave trade is told by a kidnapped White boy who is forced to work on a slave ship. *See* SOCIAL STUDIES—UNITED STATES HISTORY.

Furlong, Monica. **Juniper**. New York: Alfred A. Knopf, 1990. 198p. $12.95. ISBN 0-394-83220-5 (trade), 0-394-93220-X (lib. bdg.), 0-679-83369-2pa.

        Juniper, the town's herbalist and healer introduced in *Wise Child*, describes how she came to possess magic and power. She was a medieval princess but yearned for a different way of life, so her godmother, Euny, agreed to allow Juniper to study with her, giving her the knowledge to heal but also imparting her with magic powers that are put to the test when Juniper returns to her castle and encounters her evil Aunt Meroot, who is scheming to seize the throne. *Juniper*, written as a prequel to *Wise Child*, explains how Juniper came to be and her background, which allows her to be so wonderful with Wise Child and other townspeople who believe in her. The two books are a beautiful duo that will leave you with a wonderful feeling as well as with information about the Middle Ages and the close association between healing and magic.

————. **Wise Child**. New York: Alfred A. Knopf, 1987. 228p. $12.00. ISBN 0-394-89105-8 (trade), 0-394-99105-2 (lib. bdg.), 0-394-82598-5pa.

        When nine-year-old Wise Child is abandoned by her parents, Juniper, the local herbalist, takes her in and slowly and lovingly trains her to be a healer. During medieval times the local healer knew about herbs and "magic" and was the closest thing to a doctor. However, these people were considered witches by the church because they were perceived as a threat to the church's power. This marvelous story of Juniper's love and caring for her prodigy, Wise Child, gives a great deal of information about life at this time and the power and influence of the church. The prequel, *Juniper*, was written after *Wise Child* and explains Juniper's background and how she happened to end up in this little village.

George, Jean Craighead. **Julie of the Wolves**. In this Newbery Award-winning story Julie is lost on the North Slope of Alaska and uses her Eskimo knowledge of the wilderness to survive. She befriends a wolf pack that cares for her and helps to save her life. *See* SCIENCE.

————. **My Side of the Mountain**. Sam becomes tired of city life and goes to live in a hollow tree in the Catskill Mountains. The story is based on Jean Craighead George's firsthand knowledge of nature. *See* SCIENCE.

Hobbs, Will. **Bearstone**. New York: Atheneum, 1989. 154p. $12.95. ISBN 0-689-31496-5.

        When a social worker places Cloyd, a troubled Navajo boy, in the care of Walter, an elderly, lonely rancher in Colorado, it seems like Cloyd's last chance to turn his life around. Cloyd is caught between cultures, not really belonging to the Navajo tribe but also not comfortable with the White culture. Walter has been lonely since his wife died, but never having had children, he's apprehensive about taking Cloyd in. Still he vows to do his best. Walter makes Cloyd work but also offers him stability, a comfortable home, and fascinating tales about the surrounding gold mines. Cloyd finds solace in the mountains, where he meets up with the last grizzly and begins his crusade to save the bear. Cloyd does some dreadful things to Walter, but as time goes on the two learn to appreciate, respect, and love each other. Cloyd's love of nature helps him to better understand his culture and himself. In the sequel, *Beardance*, Cloyd continues his quest to save the grizzlies and achieves further self-discovery.

L'Engle, Madeleine. **A Wrinkle in Time**. New York: Farrar, Straus & Giroux, 1962. 203p. $14.50. ISBN 0-374-38613-7.

Meg Murry's parents are prominent scientists working on top-secret government projects. However, Meg's father has disappeared, and Meg and her unusual little brother, Charles Wallace, and her friend, Calvin O'Keefe, embark upon a fabulous "other world" adventure to locate him. Along the way they meet unusual creatures such as the hilarious Mrs. Whatsit, Mrs. Who, and Mrs. Which. They need to get from one place in time to another quickly, so they learn to "tesser," which is a way to wrinkle two places together, therefore decreasing travel distance and time. The strong theme of good versus evil unfolds as characters such as the Black Thing, the pulsing IT, and the gentle Aunt Beast are encountered. This fabulous science-fiction tale eventually led to a number of sequels, including *A Wind in the Door*, *A Swiftly Tilting Planet*, *Many Waters*, and *An Acceptable Time*. This book has stood the test of time and should be encountered by readers somewhere in their reading careers.

Lowry, Lois. **The Giver**. Boston: Houghton Mifflin, 1993. 180p. $13.95. ISBN 0-395-64566-2, 0-440-21907-8pa.

Human beings like to imagine a nirvana, where everything is perfect: no sadness, no conflict, poverty, unemployment, divorce, injustice, or inequality. However, along with no sadness comes no real happiness. The world is basically gray, with no color, no rain, no snow, and no sunshine. Jonas is a member of such a society where everything is well planned and predetermined, serene and placid. One person, the Giver, is assigned the job of remembering what it used to be like before the perfect world, and at age 12, Jonas is given this assignment. The training sessions are painful because they cause emotions and feelings, which are not experienced by the regular inhabitants. As Jonas is trained, he begins to question some of his society's practices, such as the daily pill that represses feelings, emotions, and pleasure—especially sexual pleasure. Jonas begins to question why elderly people are "released" when they are judged as flawed in some way, and he questions why the word *love* is unspoken. Baby Gabriel is having trouble adjusting and is sent to live with Jonas's family. Jonas becomes attached to him and refuses to allow him to be released, so he takes Gabriel and flees the community. The journey is difficult and arduous, and it's left up to the reader to decide whether their escape is successful. This fascinating and thought-provoking book won the Newbery Award in 1993. It makes a terrific read aloud, and interesting discussions are possible because of the many moral and ethical issues presented.

Magorian, Michelle. **Good Night, Mr. Tom**. New York: Harper & Row, 1981. 318p. $16.00. ISBN 0-06-024078-4 (trade), 0-06-024079-2 (lib. bdg.), 0-06-440174-1pa.

When World War II hit London, many children were sent out of the city to homes in the countryside to protect them from the bombings. Willie Beech, a frightened, scrawny little boy, is sent to live with a grumpy, gruff old man, Mr. Tom. Neither one wants to be together, but they have no choice, so they slowly begin to adjust to each other. As time goes on, they develop a deep love for each other. Mr. Tom discovers that Willie had been abused by his mother, but Willie now thrives with Mr. Tom's care and affection. Mr. Tom stops being a grump because he now has a purpose to his life. At the end of the war Willie is sent back to his mother, but Mr. Tom becomes concerned about him, goes to London to check on him, and discovers Willie has been severely abused and neglected again and rescues him. This warm, deeply touching story's excellent character development follows the growth of the two main characters. A great deal can also be learned about England during World War II and the war's effects on English citizens.

O'Brien, Robert. **Mrs. Frisby and the Rats of NIMH**. Illus. Zena Bernstein. New York: Atheneum, 1971. 233p. $14.95. ISBN 0-689-20651-8, 0-689-71068-2pa.

Timothy Frisby, a fragile little field mouse, is ill, and his mother needs help and advice. The owl refers her to the rats who live under the rosebush on Mr. Fitzgibbon's farm because they seem to have unusual habits and engage in daring undertakings. It's difficult, but she does get into the rats' home, only to discover it is a highly developed community with advanced technology and scientific methods in place. The social structure is also highly developed, and everyone seems to understand their place and worth in the society. The rats befriend and help Mrs. Frisby because her dead husband, Jonathan, had been their friend. As she spends time with them, she discovers the rats and her husband had been part of an experiment at the National Institute of Mental Health (NIMH) to test intelligence enhancement. The experiment worked so well with this group that they were able to escape from NIMH and set up this advanced society. This book can be enjoyed simply for the de-lightful story or studied in depth to look at social structures and societies. It makes a wonderful read aloud. Robert O'Brien's daughter, Leslie Conly, has written two enjoyable sequels: *Rasco and the Rats of NIMH* and *R. T. Margaret and the Rats of NIMH*.

Paterson, Katherine. **Bridge to Terabithia**. Illus. Donna Diamond. New York: Thomas Y. Crowell, 1977. 128p. $15.00. ISBN 0-690-04635-9, 06-440184-7pa.

Being a bit different or unusual is always difficult, especially in a small community, as Jesse Aarons knows too well. He loves to draw, which is not the accepted thing for a boy in his small farming community in the South. In fact, it's not even accepted within his family, so he compensates by practicing running and is determined to be the fastest runner in his school. When the new school year begins, his dream is threatened by a new girl, Leslie, who has moved into a house adjoining his family's farm and who is also offbeat and having trouble being accepted. They eventually race, and Leslie beats him. Jesse despises Leslie for winning, but eventually the two discover they are a lot alike and form a deep friendship. They find a secret spot across the creek and turn it into their magical kingdom, Terabithia. As the year goes on they spend wonderful times together using their vivid imaginations to invent elaborate fantasies and learning the meaning of true friendship. During Easter vacation Jesse spends a day with his teacher touring art galleries in Washington, D.C., rather than going to Terabithia with Leslie. When he returns home, he is hit with the news that Leslie had tried to cross the rain-swollen creek and drowned. This sensitive, beautifully told story of friendship is one of the best works available. The family dynamics are highly developed, and the challenge of being true to yourself and gaining acceptance by family, friends, and the community are brilliantly presented. This book is a "must read" for everyone at some time in their reading career.

———. **Jacob Have I Loved**. New York: Thomas Y. Crowell, 1980. 216p. $15.00. ISBN 0-690-04078-4 (trade), 0-690-04079-2 (lib. bdg.), 0-590-43498-5pa.

Louise and Caroline are twins growing up on an island in Chesapeake Bay in the early 1940s. Since their birth Louise has always been stronger, demanding much less attention than the sickly Caroline. Louise has learned the ways of the watermen, working side by side with her father and learning and accepting the hard life of crabbing, fishing, and culling oysters. Marvelous descriptions of the bay and working on the water are given. Louise tells the story of their lives because she is now a young woman, tired of doing all the hard work while Caroline continues to be pampered, learning music and thinking only of herself. As the story unfolds, the lives of the closely entwined girls and life on the small, remote island are revealed and well described. Louise's great desire to be wanted and appreciated is heart wrenching. She equates herself and her sister with the biblical twins, Jacob and Esau, hence the title of the book. Louise finally decides she can no longer continue this way of life and goes to college to become a doctor. Instead she graduates as a nurse-midwife and ends up in Appalachia, giving much-needed medical care to the poor people eking out a living in the mountains. One of her patients is a young woman who gives birth to twins—one very small and fragile. Immediately the healthy one is forgotten, and all attention is given to the smaller one, reminding Louise of her own story. This moving story is an important piece of literature that won the Newbery Award in 1980.

Paulsen, Gary. **Hatchet**. Brian's plane crashes and leaves him stranded in the wilds of Canada with only a hatchet to help him survive. *See* SCIENCE.

Rawls, Wilson. **Where the Red Fern Grows**. This is the story of a young boy and his two hunting dogs. *See* READ ALOUDS.

Rylant, Cynthia. **Missing May**. New York: Orchard, 1992. 89p. $14.00. ISBN 0-531-05996-0 (trade), 0-531-08596-1 (lib. bdg.), 0-440-40865-2pa.
> When Summer's parents die, she goes to live with her Aunt May and Uncle Ob. Life is great until Aunt May, a big bundle of love, dies. Summer and Uncle Ob miss her terribly, and they grieve in their own ways, trying many approaches in dealing with their loss. They finally decide to consult a medium to try to find a way to talk to Aunt May, thinking this will ease their pain. This adventure is sad and touching yet somewhat comical. This book is a valuable contribution: Though it deals with death, it has much to say about life.

Snyder, Zilpha Keatley. **The Egypt Game**. Illus. Alton Raible. New York: Atheneum, 1976. 215p. $14.00. ISBN 0-689-30006-9.
> Three neighborhood friends in Berkeley, California—Melanie; Melanie's little brother, Marshall; and April—spend a summer developing a deep friendship centered around April's interest in ancient Egypt. A local professor allows them to use an abandoned part of his backyard to play their game. They study Egypt in the local library and collect and make artifacts and store them in the professor's yard. They invent an elaborate and imaginative fantasy complete with costumes, jewelry, and artifacts based on real facts. In the fall they invite Elizabeth to join their fun, and later in the year Toby and Ken worm their way into the action. This is a wonderful story that shows the development of deep friendships, life in Berkeley during the early 1970s, and activities of bright children using their imaginations. Children of several races are represented, which is indicative of the area in which they live. A great deal of information is given about ancient Egypt, which makes the book useful when studying that time period. A sequel involving all the same children, *The Gypsy Game*, is now available. A summary is found in Chapter 5, "Greatest of the Latest."

————. **The Velvet Room**. Illus. Alton Raible. New York: Atheneum, 1978. 216p. $14.00. ISBN 0-689-30040-9, 0-440-400422pa.
> As migrant workers, Robin's family has moved around for three years. She yearns for a place to call her own and to stay there for a long time. This dream comes true when her father lands a permanent job at

the McCurdy ranch in the California Central Valley. In addition to staying in one place for a while, she meets Bridget, an elderly lady who lives in a cottage on the ranch. Bridget is a gentle, loving woman who enjoys animals and flowers and shares these with Robin. She also tells Robin about the history of the ranch and the buildings on it. Bridget gives Robin an old key that allows entry to the old, boarded-up mansion, the Palmeras House. Robin sneaks into the wonderful old house and has marvelous times exploring. She discovers her favorite place, the library, which has comfortable chairs, massive bookshelves filled with treasures, and large velvet curtains. Robin escapes to the velvet room, as she calls it, at every opportunity and discovers an old diary that uncovers an unsolved mystery.

This book begs to be read in a comfortable chair, by a cozy fire, along with a big bowl of popcorn. It's one of those beautiful "feel good" books. Share this with students who enjoy a positive, uplifting, joyful story with a bit of mystery and intrigue.

Speare, Elizabeth George. **The Witch of Blackbird Pond**. Boston: Houghton Mifflin, 1958. 249p. $13.00. ISBN 0-395-07114-3, 0-440-99577-9pa.

Life in Barbados suited Kit Tyler wonderfully until her grandfather died and she was forced to find a new home. Without sending any word, she sails to Wethersfield, Connecticut, in 1687 to live with her Aunt Rachel and her family. Upon arrival, Kit immediately has problems because she jumps off the ship to save a little girl's doll that has dropped into the water, and unbeknownst to her, anyone who can swim—especially a woman—is thought to be a witch. Kit's beautiful clothes and her unconventional upbringing are incorrect in the Puritan way of thinking, so she has to make some major adjustments in her life. She is amazed at how restricted her Aunt Rachel and her two cousins, Mercy and Judith, are. Then she meets Hannah Tupper, a lonely, elderly Quaker woman who lives outside the town by Blackbird Pond and is thought by the townspeople to be a witch. Hannah's home becomes a refuge for Kit and for an abused little girl, Prudence Cruff, whom Kit has secretly taught to read. In fact, it was Prudence's doll Kit fished from the river upon her arrival. A young man, Nathaniel Eaton, the captain's son, also comes to Hannah's when his ship, the *Dolphin,* is in. He does repairs for Hannah and helps to take care of her. Kit's uncle is appalled when he learns about her friendship with Hannah and forbids Kit to spend time there. Goodwife and Goodman Cruff, Prudence's parents, discover that Prudence can write, and they're convinced it's the Devil using her as an instrument and that Kit is a witch, causing the problem. Kit is accused of witchcraft and brought to trial, where she proves that the Devil isn't working through Prudence but that she actually knows how to read and write. Kit is freed, marries Nat and plans to spend her time traveling with him on the *Dolphin.* This 1958 Newbery Award winner is considered one of the best children's books ever written because of its excellent character development, historical accuracy, and beautiful story. It is an excellent book to use when studying early America and the Puritan time period.

Steinbeck, John. **The Red Pony**. Illus. Wesley Dennis. New York: Bantam, 1938, reissued 1988. 120p. $16.00. ISBN 0-553-278363, 067-081-2854, 0-67-059184X.

>   Jody Tiflin's life on a ranch in the California Central Valley is great for a young boy because he has room to roam. But with few other children around, he is fairly lonely. He knows how to care for the animals, and his dog, Doubletree Mutt, is his constant companion, but Jody's greatest desire is to own a pony of his own. His father, a rather strict, unemotional man, gives in and presents him with a beautiful red pony colt. Jody is ecstatic and vows to take good care of the pony, which he names Gabilan, after the mountains surrounding their ranch. The pony becomes the most important thing in Jody's life, and under the firm but loving tutelage of the ranch hand, Billy Buck, Jody learns how to care for the pony properly, causing it to thrive. However, Gabilan is left out in the corral one day when Jody is at school, and Billy Buck is not able to put the pony into the barn when it starts raining. The pony's lungs become infected. Despite all Billy Buck's and Jody's efforts, it dies. Jody is devastated, but through death he learns a great deal about life. This sensitive, caring story makes a wonderful read aloud.

Taylor, Mildred D. **Roll of Thunder, Hear My Cry**. The story of the Logans, a Black family living in Mississippi during the Great Depression, is a socially significant work. *See* SOCIAL STUDIES—UNITED STATES HISTORY.

Taylor, Theodore. **The Cay**. New York: Avon Books, 1969. 144p. $10.95. ISBN 0-380-01003-8pa.

>   In setting this story the author explains how the oil refineries on the island of Curacao supply much of the oil for tankers and airplanes for the Allied Forces in Europe during World War II. But it becomes dangerous, and the mother of one family living on the island insists on returning to Virginia, leaving the father, the head of the refinery, behind. The woman and her son, Phillip, travel on a Dutch ship, the *S.S. Hato*, bound for Panama. Phillip's father feels they will be safe on this ship because it only carries pumps—nothing concerning the war. However, they are torpedoed, and Phillip and his mother end up on different life rafts. Phillip is hit on the head by a piece of the sinking ship but is saved by his life-raft companion, an old Black man named Timothy. Phillip is repulsed by Timothy because he's been taught that Blacks are different and bad. Due to the head injury, Phillip loses his eyesight, but during their long, arduous journey to safety, Timothy cares for Phillip and risks his life several times in one exciting episode after the next. Phillip is totally dependent on Timothy and slowly but surely learns color blindness. They make camp on a cay and wait to be rescued until a vicious hurricane arrives and Timothy is killed. Phillip is eventually rescued, and after operations, his sight is restored. But his life is rich and full because of his experiences with the shunned Black man, Timothy. This exciting, touching, and thought-provoking story has stood the test of time.

————. **Timothy of the Cay**. New York: Harcourt Brace & Company, 1993. 161p. $13.95. ISBN 0-15-288358-4, 0-380-72119-8pa.

It took Theodore Taylor 24 years to do it, but after much begging from children around the world and finally his own children, he wrote a prequel-sequel to *The Cay*. Using alternating chapters, he tells the stories of Timothy and Phillip. Phillip's story is the sequel, describing the events after his rescue from the cay, while Timothy's story is the prequel, telling about his life as a little boy until his death on the cay. Phillip has an operation that restores his sight, and his family returns to Curacao, stopping along the way at the cay where Phillip and Timothy had lived. Phillip visits Timothy's grave and says his final good-byes. Timothy's story begins in 1884, when, as a young boy on a Caribbean island, he lives in utmost poverty with his Tante Hannah. He fibs about his age and is hired as a deckhand on a ship, thus beginning his difficult life on the water, often suffering discrimination because of his race. However, because of his determination and spirit he lives a full life that ends with the hurricane on the cay. The stories are well told and touching, and anyone who enjoys *The Cay* will love this prequel-sequel.

Chapter 3

ENGLISH—USE OF LANGUAGE

It's fun to play around with words and language usage, and the books in this section do just that. They can be used to teach a particular concept or can simply be enjoyed for their humorous presentation.

Agee, Jon. **Go Hang a Salami! I'm a Lasagna Hog! And Other Palindromes**. New York: Farrar, Straus & Giroux, 1991. 73p. $12.00. ISBN 0-374-33473-0.

Palindromes are words that are the same backward and forward and can be as simple as *wow*, *Otto*, or *noon*. However, Jon Agee goes the extra mile and comes up with entire sentences that are palindromes— some of them quite long, as seen in the title of the book. He adds line drawings to the sayings to make them even crazier. As you page through this book you'll find yourself shaking your head wondering how he came up with these. Some examples are "Did mom pop? Mom did," "A car, a man, a maraca," and "Mr. Owl ate my metal worm." Students can have fun with these and attempt to make their own.

Avi. **"Who Was That Masked Man, Anyway?"** Frankie and Mario are hooked on radio shows in 1945, causing them to become involved in hilarious situations. The entire book is written in dialogue, making it an excellent source to use as an example of conversational writing. *See* UNIQUE PRESENTATIONS.

Carroll, Lewis. **Jabberwocky**. Illus. from the Disney Archives. New York: Disney Press, 1992. $14.00. ISBN 1-56282-245-4 (trade), 1-56282-246-2 (lib. bdg.).

A prime example of playing around with words and word sounds is the poem "Jabberwocky" from *Alice's Adventures in Wonderland*. Some of the words are real, but many are made up, and at first glance the phrases make absolutely no sense. However, by reading the poem out loud and adding voice inflections, the nonsense begins to take shape and have meaning, and it's possible to determine the story being told. This is a marvelous example of how word usage and placement and parts of speech work together to fashion meaning. This particular rendition includes brightly painted illustrations from the Disney archives to help tell the story.

Gwynne, Fred. **A Chocolate Moose for Dinner**. New York: Simon & Schuster, 1976. 47p. $10.50. ISBN 0-525-61545-8, 0-525-62317-5pa.

A little girl hears her parents say things that have double meanings—such as having chocolate mousse for dinner—and she pictures a large, luscious-looking chocolate moose sitting across the table from her. This work is filled with 20 crazy uses of homonyms that will make the reader chuckle and learn. Each phrase is on a two-page spread with a large cartoonlike picture depicting the phrase. The final item says "Stories like these drive me up a wall!" and it pictures the girl in a little car zooming up the living room wall. Students will have fun thinking of their own homonym phrases and illustrating them in a humorous fashion.

————. **The King Who Rained**. New York: Simon & Schuster, 1970. 47p. $10.50. ISBN 0-13-516212-2, 0-13-516170-3pa.

A little girl hears her parents say things that can have a double meaning, and she pictures them differently from the way the grown-ups intended. For example, Mommy says she has a "frog in her throat," and the little girl pictures her mother with a large, green frog sitting in Mommy's mouth. Each of the 19 entries consists of a phrase using a homonym along with a two-page illustration depicting the little girl's humorous interpretation of the phrase. Some of the phrases in this book are a bit obscure and might need a little explanation, such as the lambs that "gamble on the lawn."

————. **A Little Pigeon Toad**. New York: Simon & Schuster Books for Young Readers, 1988. Unpaged. $11.95. ISBN 0-671-66659-2, 0-440-84798-2pa.

Each of the 22 items gives a phrase that contains a homonym or a figure of speech that a little girl hears her parents say and gives her interpretation and her own spelling of that phrase. She says that her father says that "tennis rackets should be taught," so she has three tennis rackets sitting in chairs facing a large blackboard with the little girl giving tennis instruction. Lists of homonyms can be gleaned from the Fred Gwynne books, and students can practice coming up with their own humorous phrases and illustrations.

————. **The Sixteen Hand Horse**. New York: Prentice-Hall Books for Young Readers, 1980. Unpaged. $6.00. ISBN 0-13-811522-2, 0-13-811456-0pa.

A young girl hears her parents say phrases that contain homonyms, and she interprets the ideas and spellings using the wrong homonyms, which makes the phrase humorous. Author Fred Gwynne also uses some idioms in this work, so examples of idioms as well as homonyms can be discussed. The girl hears her mother say "her nose is running," so she pictures her mother's nose with two little legs running down the hallway. A note of caution: One of the entries says Daddy is opposed to joining "the tennis club because all the members are wasps." This could be interpreted as a racial slur, so care needs to be taken. Students love the Gwynne books, but they can be puzzling to children whose first language is not English. Using these books is a good jumping-off place for creating student work using similar phrases.

Heller, Ruth. **A Cache of Jewels and Other Collective Nouns**. New York: Scholastic, 1987. Unpaged. $10.95. ISBN 0-590-42586-2pa.

> Collective nouns are explained and presented in a colorful, humorous manner. Each two-page spread gives examples of collective nouns—such as a pride of lions, an army of ants, a parcel of penguins, and a coven of witches—all told in rhyme. The bold, splashy drawings help to illustrate the concept and create a visual feast. On the last page the author explains collective nouns and gives their history.

————. **Kites Sail High: A Book About Verbs**. New York: Grosset & Dunlap, 1988. 41p. $14.50. ISBN 0-448-10480-6, 0-590-43764-Xpa.

> This is a great way to have some fun while learning about verbs. The first half of the book gives examples of verbs, told in rhyme, along with large, colorful illustrations that actively describe the verbs in action. The second half of the book shows specific types of verbs, how verbs are used, tenses, moods, voices, contractions, and everything you always wanted and needed to know about verbs. This is an exciting way to learn about verbs and see them in action.

————. **Many Luscious Lollipops: A Book About Adjectives**. New York: Grosset & Dunlap, 1989. 44p. $14.50. ISBN 0-448-03151-5, 0-590-43763-1pa.

> The study of adjectives has been made interesting and easy to understand with this colorful rhyming work. Every aspect of adjectives is discussed, making them come alive with the help of humorous, wild, and splashy artwork. Adjectives are capitalized in the text, making it easier to identify them.

————. **Merry-Go-Round: A Book About Nouns**. New York: Grosset & Dunlap, 1990. 42p. $14.50. ISBN 0-448-40085-5, 0-590-45677-6pa.

> Nouns are presented in detail and told in rhyme, with the help of bold, splashy illustrations. Each noun is in bold print, while the type of noun is written in capital letters. This could be used as a textbook when teaching nouns because it covers all the basic information about them. It can also be used as entertainment because of the outstanding illustrations and the rhyming text.

Rosen, Michael. **Walking the Bridge of Your Nose**. Illus. Chloë Cheese. New York: Kingfisher, 1995. 61p. $12.95. ISBN 1-85697-596-7.

> Anyone who has any interest in language and the fun things we can do with it needs to use this book. It is jam-packed with tongue twisters, riddles, puns, word games, wordplay, humorous rhymes, limericks, and

word puzzles. Each page is a feast of language play that will have the readers and listeners chuckling and shaking their heads and marveling at the cleverness of each entry. The collection is divided into sections that give a good indication of the madness within that section: "Mind Manglers," "Silly Patter," "Nursery Crime," "Sound Bites," "Riddle-Me-Re," "Tombstone Tomfoolery," "Nonsense," "Crazy Chains," "English Class," "Baloney & Bunkum," "Preposterous Puns," and "Mind Benders." The pieces in this book beg to be read aloud, but you should practice beforehand, because the tongue can easily get tangled in this display of wacky words.

Terban, Marvin. **I Think I Thought, and Other Tricky Verbs**. Illus. Giulio Maestro. New York: Clarion Books, 1984. 64p. $8.75. ISBN 0-89919-231-9, 0-89919-290-4pa.

Regular verbs are quite easy, but irregular verbs sometimes need more practice. Thirty commonly used irregular verbs are presented in this book in a humorous manner that will help make the job more fun. The irregular verb is presented on one side of the page along with a humorous picture, and the other side of the page is the past tense of the verb along with a descriptive picture. Each sentence is alliterative, and the two sentences rhyme, as with "Charlie chooses chowder, not chop suey" and "Chiquita chose cheesecake that was gooey." The last page lists 30 verbs found in the book, along with their past tense and past participle, making this a valuable tool when studying verbs.

————. **In a Pickle, and Other Funny Idioms**. Illus. Giulio Maestro. New York: Clarion Books, 1983. 64p. $12.50. ISBN 0-89919-153-3.

Thirty common idioms such as "butterflies in the stomach," "bury your head in the sand," and "in one ear and out the other" are presented on two-page spreads. On one side the idiom is used in a sentence with a humorous picture to help explain it, and on the other side the idiom is written out along with its meaning and a paragraph or two giving further explanation and a bit of history when possible. It is often confusing for students learning English or about English to understand idioms because they are groups of words that don't mean what they say. Therefore, this is an excellent tool to use with those children.

————. **Mad As a Wet Hen! And Other Funny Idioms**. Illus. Giulio Maestro. New York: Clarion Books, 1987. 64p. $12.50. ISBN 0-89919-478-8, 0-89919-479-6pa.

More than 130 common idioms are arranged according to such categories as animals, body parts, feelings, colors, food, and hats. Each idiom is presented in a sentence along with a small, humorous illustration, a paragraph explaining the idiom, and, if known, the background of the idiom. An alphabetical listing of all the idioms in the book is given in the back of the book, and a bibliography of other idiom books is included. This collection is a valuable tool to be used when studying idioms, but it can also be used as a reference tool when an explanation for an idiom is needed.

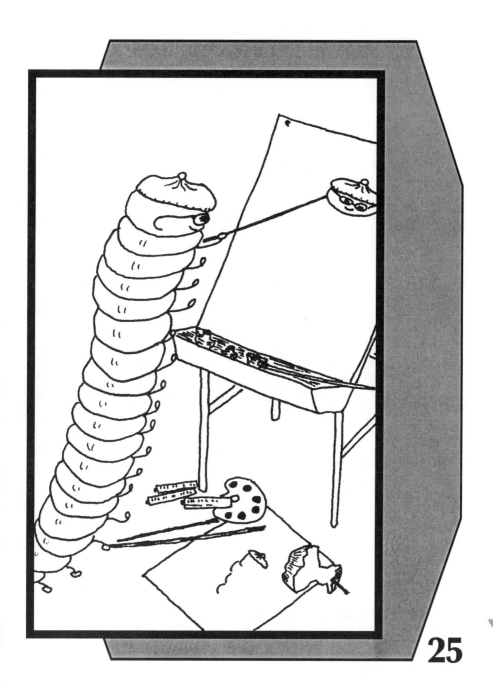

Chapter 4
FINE ARTS

A variety of books are cited in this section that includes various aspects of art from around the world, music, artists, how-to books, and architecture. The fine arts are important by themselves, but they also make an interesting and fun tie-in with other curricula. Hopefully the books in this section will help accomplish this goal.

———

Ada, Alma Flor. **Gathering the Sun: An Alphabet in Spanish and English**. Trans. Rosa Zubizarreta, illus. Simón Silva. Excellent examples of vibrant Mexican-American artwork. *See* MULTICULTURAL.

Angelou, Maya. **Life Doesn't Frighten Me**. Illus. Jean-Michel Basquiat. This work includes excellent artwork by Jean-Michel Basquiat, along with his biography. *See* POETRY.

Bateson-Hill, Margaret. **Lao Lao of Dragon Mountain**. Chinese text Manyee Wan, illus. Francesca Pelizzoli, paper cuts Sha-Liu Qu. New York: Stewart, Tabori & Chang, 1996. 29p. $8.50. ISBN 1-89988-364-9.

> This multifaceted book can be used in many ways, but one of its uses can be to teach Chinese paper cutting. An old Chinese woman, Lao Lao, spends many happy moments cutting shapes from paper for the village children. But her fame spreads, and the greedy emperor hears about her. He has his men capture her, take her to a dismal room, and demand that she cut jewels from an enormous stack of paper. The mountain's Ice Dragon sees her dilemma, turns the guards and the emperor into ice, and frees Lao Lao, who rides on the dragon's back, cutting as she goes. In spring she puts pink blossoms on the trees. In the summer she fills the fields with flowers. In the winter she makes snowflakes. The pages are filled with marvelous illustrations depicting the text and with the Chinese translation of the story, large Chinese-language characters, and a delicate drawing of the paper cuts described. Large, detailed directions for paper cuts of a butterfly, a flower, a snowflake, and a dragon are given at the end of the book, along with an explanation about the history and importance of paper cuts in China. This book is valuable because it can be used when discussing Chinese language, folklore, history, culture, and art.

Cha, Dia. **Dia's Story Cloth: The Hmong People's Journey of Freedom**. A Hmong family's life story is told with the help of a stitched wall hanging. *See* MULTICULTURAL.

Demi. **One Grain of Rice: A Mathematical Folktale**. Excellent examples of Indian art are used in this retelling of the multiplication of the grains of rice. *See* MATHEMATICS.

Drew. Helen. **My First Music Book**. New York: Dorling Kindersley, 1993. 46p. $12.95. ISBN 1-56458-215-9.
 If you ever have a need for a book showing how to make musical instruments from everyday items, this is for you. In true Dorling Kindersley fashion, bold, large, colorful pictures show all the supplies needed for each instrument, and detailed directions explain how to make and decorate each one. The pages are large with a minimum amount of text, so the step-by-step directions are easy to follow. By using this book you can make shakers of many varieties, tambourines, drums, guiros (rasping noisemakers), a triangle, a xylophone, bells, panpipes, a bubble organ, horn pipes, stringed instruments of several varieties, and a banjo. The title gives the impression this is a book for young children, and indeed, some of the children pictured are of elementary age. However, this is misleading, because the information is appropriate for students of all ages. This can serve as a valuable tool when a unit on sound is studied in science. Students can have lots of fun making and playing musical instruments while learning about sound.

Gravett, Christopher. **The Knight's Handbook: How to Become a Champion in Shining Armor**. New York: Cobblehill Books, 1997. 29p. $13.99. ISBN 0-525-65241-8.
 This book is made to order for students hooked on the Middle Ages who love to create and reenact episodes from that time period. It presents a paragraph or two about an aspect of the Middle Ages, such as armor and weapons. It then gives careful, exact directions, complete with color photographs, telling how to make a helmet. Directions are also given for making a sword, a shield of arms, a castle, jousting knights, a board game, and a catapult. It also includes a recipe for honey toasts with pine nuts, a medieval dish, in the "Food" section. This is a terrific how-to book for the Middle Ages.

Krull, Kathleen. **Lives of the Artists: Masterpieces, Messes (and What the Neighbors Thought)**. Illus. Kathryn Hewitt. New York: Harcourt Brace & Company, 1995. 96p. $19.00. ISBN 0-15-200103-4.
 Interesting and often humorous biographies of 20 world-famous artists representing a variety of countries, artistic styles, and time periods are presented in this concise yet informative book. Each artist is depicted by a full-page color illustration, with the head being the most prominent part of the picture. The clothing and other articles in the illustration symbolize the artist. A three- to five-page biography follows that includes a great deal of information and is written in a lighthearted yet informative manner. At the end of each article, additional interesting facts are given in the section "Artworks." A list of artistic terms is given at the end

of the book along with an index and a bibliography. The artists included are Leonardo da Vinci, Michelangelo Buonarroti, Pieter Brueghel, Sofonisba Anguisciola, Rembrandt van Rijn, Katsushika Hokusai, Mary Cassatt, Vincent van Gogh, Käthe Kollwitz, Henri Matisse, Pablo Picasso, Marc Chagall, Marcel Duchamp, Georgia O'Keeffe, William H. Johnson, Salvador Dali, Isamu Noguchi, Diego Rivera, Frida Kahlo, and Andy Warhol.

————. **Lives of the Musicians: Good Times, Bad Times (and What the Neighbors Thought)**. Illus. Kathryn Hewitt. New York: Harcourt Brace & Company, 1993. 96p. $18.95. ISBN 0-15-248010-2.

Twenty musicians from different countries, historical periods, and musical styles are presented as real, often eccentric, sometimes amusing but successful people, important to the world. Each musician is depicted in a full-page color illustration, with the head being the most prominent part of the picture. The clothing indicates the time period and instrument associated with that musician. Three pages of biographical information present the musician in a real and somewhat comical fashion. A great deal of information is given in a compressed article, making it useful and entertaining. A section at the end of each article, "Musical Notes," gives additional interesting facts—often funny and fascinating. The musicians presented are Antonio Vivaldi, Johann Sebastian Bach, Wolfgang Amadeus Mozart, Ludwig van Beethoven, Frédéric Chopin, Giuseppe Verdi, Clara Schumann, Stephen Foster, Johannes Brahms, Pyotr Tchaikovsky, William Gilbert and Arthur Sullivan, Erik Satie, Scott Joplin, Charles Ives, Igor Stravinsky, Nadia Boulanger, Sergey Prokofiev, George Gershwin, and Woody Guthrie. A list of musical terms, an index, and a bibliography are included.

Lobel, Anita. **The Dwarf Giant**. New York: Greenwillow, 1996. Unpaged. $16.00. ISBN 0-688-14407-1.

A quiet, ancient Japanese kingdom is turned upside down by the arrival of a dwarf who entertains and makes merry. The prince falls under the dwarf's spell, but the princess becomes alarmed as the merriment turns into havoc and destruction. She enlists the help of the people of the kingdom, and they fight off and destroy the dwarf, whose sole purpose had been to destroy and take over the kingdom. The story is entertaining, but the outstanding thing about this book is the artwork. Japanese art is beautifully presented as Anita Lobel illustrates ancient Japan with colorful, bold paintings. The action—much of it comical—would work well as a play, further depicting ancient Japan.

Lorenz, Albert, with Joy Schleh. **Metropolis: Ten Cities, Ten Centuries**. The art, architecture, life, and culture of ten major cities of the world from the eleventh to the twentieth centuries are vividly displayed. *See* SOCIAL STUDIES—ANCIENT AND EARLY CULTURES.

Nichol, Barbara. **Beethoven Lives Upstairs**. Illus. Scott Cameron. A biography of Ludwig van Beethoven is told using letters written between a boy and his uncle. *See* UNIQUE PRESENTATIONS.

Panzer, Nora, ed. **Celebrate America: In Poetry and Art**. New York: Hyperion Books for Children, 1994. 96p. ISBN 1-56282-664-6 (trade), 1-56282-665-4 (lib. bdg.).

> Famous pieces of artwork from the National Museum of American Art, Smithsonian Institution, and some of the best of American poetry are brought together to celebrate the American experience. It's divided into five sections, beginning with "A Place of Eagles," which vividly shows and tells about our country from the deserts to the mountains to the prairies. "Remembering the Sky You Were Born Under" pays tribute to the various groups of people who have shaped this country, including Native Americans, the pioneers, African-Americans, and refugees from many lands. Section three, "A Great Pulse Beating," shows various people and their work, such as the homesteaders, the vaqueros, people who work assembly lines, builders, farmers, and city dwellers. "Lift Every Voice" celebrates those who fought for freedom and includes the poem Maya Angelou read for Bill Clinton's presidential inauguration, "On the Pulse of Morning." The final section, "Timeless Is the Wheel," shows life in America, including small towns, schools, cowboys, baseball, football, and jazz. Biographical notes about the writers and artists are included. The poetry and artwork fit together perfectly to celebrate America and its many wonders, making this a beautiful, useful tool when teaching art, poetry, and American history.

Peterson, Gail. **Greg Hildebrandt's Book of Three-Dimensional Dragons**. Five large and colorful dragons literally pop out of this outstanding pop-up book. These could be used when constructing dragons or as examples when designing pop-up books. *See* UNIQUE PRESENTATIONS.

Preiss, Byron, ed. **The Best Children's Books in the World: A Treasury of Illustrated Stories**. This collection of illustrated stories from around the world gives excellent examples of art from around the world. *See* MULTICULTURAL.

Reddix, Valerie. **Dragon Kite of the Autumn Moon**. Illus. Jean Tseng and Mou-sien Tseng. Beautiful illustrations of dragon kites accompany this tale based on an ancient Chinese tradition. *See* SOCIAL STUDIES—ANCIENT AND EARLY CULTURES.

Sola, Michele. **Angela Weaves a Dream: The Story of a Young Maya Artist**. Photo. Jeffrey Jay Foxx. New York: Hyperion Books for Children, 1996. 47p. $16.89. ISBN 0-7868-2060-8.

> Weaving is as important to the Mayans now as it has been since the beginning of their civilization. Angela is excited because she learns that young girls as well as the adult women are now allowed to enter the Weaving Contest, an annual event of great importance. We follow Angela as she prepares to enter the contest, beginning with the sheep shearing, the carding, cleaning, dying, and spinning of the wool. Each step is presented with text as well as outstanding color photographs, capturing the painstaking and time-consuming process of readying the wool. Angela is then taught the seven sacred weaving designs of her town, San Andres. These ancient designs carry stories passed on by the oldest family members. Each of the seven designs is illustrated and its story told as the weaving proceeds in this gentle, beautiful story about an age-old tradition, captured with words and photographs. The art of weaving is clearly and beautifully described, and the author's and photographer's notes at the back of the book describe the background and importance of the weavings in the Mayan culture.

Stanley, Diane. **Leonardo da Vinci**. An illustrated biography of Leonardo da Vinci. *See* BIOGRAPHIES.

Van Zandt, Eleanor. **A History of the United States Through Art**. New York: Thomson Learning, 1996. 48p. ISBN 1-56847-443-1.

> In a perfect linking of curricula, this book tells the history of the United States using famous paintings of various time periods and events. Each painting is described, and the story behind it is told along with historical information. It begins with the first Americans with a painting by John White, "The Manner of Their Fishing." It continues by showing the Plymouth Colony, "Pilgrims Going to Church," by George Henry Boughton; farm life, "The Residence of David Twining, 1787," by Edward Hicks; "Boston Tea Party," a lithograph by Currier and Ives; "The Declaration of Independence," by John Trumbull; and "Washington Crossing the Delaware," by Emanuel Leutze. It continues with 17 more important artworks, ending with World War II depicted with "Signs," a screen print by Robert Rauschenberg. The description next to each piece includes the present location of the work. A glossary and a time line make this a useful and informative work for historical purposes as well as art appreciation.

Wilson, Elizabeth B. **Bibles and Bestiaries: A Guide to Illuminated Manuscripts**. New York: Farrar, Straus & Giroux, 1994. 64p. $25.00. ISBN 0-374-30685-0.

> Only the very wealthy and the church were able to own books during the Middle Ages because of the painstaking task of copying each word in longhand, with all artwork also done by hand. As time went on,

producing a "manuscript," the Latin word for *book* because it was written "by hand," became an advanced art form. The paintings, when decorated with real gold or silver, were called illuminations, from the Latin word for *light*. Illuminated manuscripts were beautiful artwork but also a fascinating way of recording the happenings during that time period. Many of these manuscripts have been preserved, giving us a marvelous look at the past. This book discusses and describes illuminated manuscripts in detail, showing how the books were made, how the drawings were done, which topics were the "best-sellers," and how the invention of printing presses changed things. Each page contains several outstanding examples of manuscripts and illuminations, their meanings, and how they were made. All the illustrations are taken from New York's Pierpont Morgan Library, which contains the largest collection of illuminated manuscripts outside Europe. An informative write-up about the Pierpont Morgan Library is included, along with a glossary and a key to the illustrations. This is an exceptional source to use when studying art history or the Middle Ages.

Wisniewski, David. **The Warrior and the Wise Man**. Excellent examples of paper-cut artwork are used to help tell the ancient Japanese story. *See* SOCIAL STUDIES—ANCIENT AND EARLY CULTURES.

Chapter 5

GREATEST OF THE LATEST

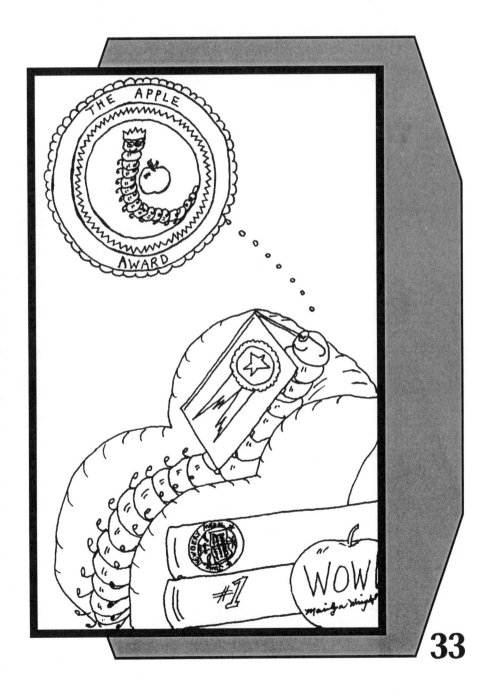

Keeping up with the latest in children's literature is exciting yet a challenge because, luckily for us, new books are being marketed daily. The titles included were new at the time of this publication, and in future updates of this book, this section will change dramatically. Some of the selections are by our favorite authors, and some are new authors with a fresh approach, giving a mix of high-quality literature.

Avi. **The Barn**. New York: Orchard, 1994. 106p. $13.95. ISBN 0-531-08711(trade), 0-531-06861-7 (lib. bdg.), 0-380-72562-2pa.
> After their father suffers a stroke, then called "palsy," Benjamin, Nettie, and Harrison must take care of him as well as the farm in the Oregon Territory in the 1850s. Ben, the youngest, is assigned to take care of the helpless father, which at first is difficult and disgusting. Their once strong, wonderful father is mute and helpless, needing to be fed, cared for, and cleaned. As time goes on, Ben learns to communicate with the speechless man and gets the notion that if their father's dream to build a barn came true, he would recover. The three children do all the normal, hard farmwork as well as fell the trees, split the logs, build the foundation, and construct the barn. Ben puts his father into the wheelbarrow so that he can go outside to watch the progress of the barn. This tender story shows pioneer life as well as strong family love, resourcefulness, and hope.

————. **Beyond the Western Sea: Book One, Escape from Home**. European immigration to the United States is the main topic with lots of intrigue and adventure included. *See* SOCIAL STUDIES—UNITED STATES HISTORY.

————. **Beyond the Western Sea: Book Two, Lord Kirkle's Money**. This is a continuation of Book One, with the immigrants finally getting to the United States and becoming involved with the Industrial Age and textile mills of Lowell, Massachusetts. *See* SOCIAL STUDIES—UNITED STATES HISTORY.

Choi, Sook Nyul. **Gathering of Pearls**. This is the third book in the saga of Sookan Bak's life in Korea during and after the Korean War. In this volume she travels to New York City to study. *See* MULTICULTURAL.

Curtis, Christopher. **The Watsons Go to Birmingham—1963**. A middle-class Black family becomes involved in the Civil Rights movement. *See* SOCIAL STUDIES—UNITED STATES HISTORY.

Cushman, Karen. **The Ballad of Lucy Whipple**. New York: Clarion Books, 1996. 195p. $13.95. ISBN 0-395-72806-1.

    Lucy Whipple's pa and ma dreamed of pulling up stakes in Massachusetts and trying their luck in California's goldfields. Pa died, but Ma did not forget the dream. Instead, she gathered up her five children and headed West. All along the way people warn her to go back, but she continues to pursue the dream and ends up in a dusty tent town, Lucky Diggins. The oldest daughter, California Morning Whipple, changes her name to Lucy and refuses to accept this nonsense. She dreams about her previous home, real food, and a real house, and most of all she wants a school and books. She can dream all she wants, but the family is destined to stay in Lucky Diggins to endure, experience, and finally enjoy the rough-and-tumble life of the California mining settlement. Reading this book is a great way to experience life in the California goldfields.

DeFelice, Cynthia. **The Apprenticeship of Lucas Whitaker**. An outbreak of tuberculosis in the mid-1800s in Connecticut is met with superstition and fear rather than scientific knowledge and reasoning. Lucas is apprenticed to a doctor fighting to find a cure for the disease rather than curing it with the macabre practices taking place in his community. *See* SCIENCE.

Fitzgerald, John D. **The Great Brain Is Back**. Illus. Diane deGroat. New York: Dial Books for Young Readers, 1995. 121p. $14.95. ISBN 0-8037-1346-0 (trade), 0-8037-1347-9 (lib. bdg.).

    The Great Brain books have delighted readers for nearly 30 years with all eight of the books in the series being read again and again. After John Fitzgerald's death, manuscripts of more stories about J. D. and his big brother, Tom, were found, with enough stories to assemble one last book. This time Tom is 13 and eager to get the attention of Polly Reagan. However, he continues where he left off when it comes to conniving, swindling, and outwitting all who come in contact with him. Growing up in Utah in the late 1800s in a small town could have been boring, but Tom saw to it that some excitement was always at hand. Great Brain books make great read alouds because of the boys' crazy adventures. The other titles in the series are *The Great Brain*, *More Adventures of the Great Brain*, *Me and My Little Brain*, *The Great Brain at the Academy*, *The Great Brain Reforms*, *The Return of the Great Brain*, and *The Great Brain Does It Again*.

Hautman, Pete. **Mr. Was**. New York: Simon & Shuster Books for Young Readers, 1996. 216p. $16.00. ISBN 0-689-81068-7.

After Jack's grandfather's death, Jack and his parents spend time in small-town Memory, Minnesota, in his grandfather's old house. Jack discovers a magical door and goes through it as a way of escaping his parents' violent fighting, which is brought on by his father's alcoholism. Each time Jack goes through the door he ends up in a different era with different people—some his ancestors. On his last trip through the door he finds himself on Guadalcanal during World War II. The resulting psychological damage causes him to be confined in a secret government asylum for many years. Science-fiction fans will love this one, though reading it more than once may help in putting all the pieces together in this science fiction-mystery-thriller.

Hobbs, Will. **Far North**. High adventure takes place when a small plane crashes in the wilds of Canada and the passengers attempt to survive an Arctic winter. *See* SCIENCE.

————. **Ghost Canoe**. New York: Morrow Junior Books, 1997. 193p. $15.00. ISBN 0-688-14193-5.

Fourteen-year-old Nathan MacAllister loves the challenge of working like a man with his father, the lighthouse keeper, on Tatoosh Island, Washington, in the 1870s. However, the climate on the island is making his mother ill, so he goes to live on the mainland with her until she recovers. While there, he is determined to solve the mystery of a shipwreck that involved the murder of the captain. He also becomes close to the Makah Indians, learning their customs, foods, survival techniques, and way of life. This is Will Hobbs's first mystery, but it is jammed with the history of the Northwest, seafaring lore, Native American culture, and science as well as suspense.

Howe, James. **The Watcher**. New York: Atheneum Books for Young Readers, 1997. $15.00. ISBN 0-689-80186-6.

Day after day a solitary, silent girl sits at the top of the steps at the beach showing no emotion whatsoever. Evan and Callie, vacationing with their family, are haunted by the mysterious girl, who Evan names the Watcher. But they continue playing on the beach trying to ignore her. Chris, the lifeguard, a gorgeous hunk, tries to befriend the silent girl, without success. The girl's thoughts are revealed through her fantasies about an imaginary girl who is captive on an island and about Evan and Callie, imagining they have the perfect family. Her fantasies are written in italics, setting them apart from the other action at the beach. What the girl doesn't know is that Callie has nightmares, and Evan is her protector because their "perfect family" is falling apart, with the mother and father having marital problems. Chris looks marvelous on the outside, but in actuality he's aimless, not knowing where his life is going, and a fellow lifeguard, Jenny, is caring for him and trying to guide him. James Howe masterfully weaves a complicated story about people who seem normal on the outside but who, when known more intimately, have their private demons. The only one outwardly disturbed is the Watcher, and her fantasies become more wild and complicated. Her deep secret is finally revealed when Chris and Evan call the police after Evan witnesses severe abuse by the girl's father. Her demons begin to fall away when she is finally able to say the words *My father hurts me*. This is a haunting, well-written, complicated story—quite different from Howe's lighthearted Bunnicula stories.

Konigsburg, E. L. **The View from Saturday**. New York: Atheneum Books for Young Readers, 1996. 163p. $16.00. ISBN 0-689-80993-X.

Mrs. Olinski, a wheelchair-bound sixth-grade teacher, chooses Noah, Nadia, Julian, and Ethan for the Academic Bowl team. Each character, with his or her unique talents, personality, and story, develops slowly but thoroughly as the story progresses. As Mrs. Olinski molds and trains this odd group, her own healing begins, helping her to overcome the tragic automobile accident that killed her husband and left her handicapped. The group's road to triumph is humorous, exciting, and suspenseful. As an addendum, the 15 Academic Bowl questions are listed, along with the correct answers. This well-developed story earned E. L. Konigsburg the 1996 Newbery Award.

Mooney, Bel. **The Voices of Silence**. New York: Delacorte Press, 1997. 181p. $14.95. ISBN 0-385-32326-3.

Imagine living under a suppressive government that watches your movements and causes you to suspect everyone as being a possible "securitate," or secret police. Imagine never having enough to eat, never having chocolate or fruit, and having to stand in long lines early in the morning with the hopes of buying a stale loaf of bread. Imagine never having new clothes because they simply aren't available or enough heat in the winter because of a lack of fuel. This is the world of Flora Popescu in Romania in 1989 under the rule of Nicolae Ceausescu before the fall of Communism. Flora is experiencing the feelings and desires of a typical teenager, but the government's strong hand gets in the way. A new boy, Daniel, arrives at school with unheard of items—chewing gum, meat in his sandwiches, and chocolate. She wants to be friends with him but knows she needs to be suspect of him. Her growing friendship with Daniel causes a rift with her lifelong friend, Alys, and when it becomes apparent that even her parents are hiding deep secrets, Flora's life becomes even more complicated. Her curiosity takes her to the main palace square the day Ceausescu is overpowered, and she witnesses the tanks plowing through thousands of people, killing and maiming in their wake. The Romanian revolution is experienced through Flora and her family and friends. This powerful book presents a topic rarely dealt with in children's literature. It is well written, holds the reader's attention intently, and provides a window to a world quite unlike ours.

Myers, Walter Dean. **Slam!** This is the story of a Black inner-city basketball player coming of age. *See* SPORTS AND GAMES.

Naylor, Phyllis Reynolds. **Shiloh Season**. New York: Atheneum Books for Young Readers, 1996. 120p. $15.00. ISBN 0-689-80647-7.
> In this sequel to Phyllis Naylor's 1991 Newbery Award winner, *Shiloh*, Marty continues to enjoy his dog, Shiloh, but the vengeful neighbor, Judd, remains a threat and catches Marty and his friend, David, snooping on his property. To gain revenge, Judd threatens to hunt and kill Shiloh. The boys become involved in several adventures while keeping Shiloh from harm, yet manage to keep their trespassing on Judd's property a secret. It would be helpful to read *Shiloh* first to best enjoy this sequel. The concluding volume of the Shiloh trilogy, *Saving Shiloh* (ISBN 0-689-81460-7) is now available.

Paterson, Katherine. **Jip: His Story**. New York: Lodestar Books, 1996. 181p. $15.99. ISBN 0-525-6743-4.
> As a small child, Jip was brought to the town's poor farm in Vermont after he fell from a wagon and no one claimed him. Even though he is an orphan and receives little attention from the overseer and his wife, he has a positive outlook on life and is satisfied working on the farm that supports the home. He takes care of the animals and others in the home, including a raging lunatic, Put, and learns how to calm him. He is finally allowed to go to school, where the teacher and her Quaker friend, Luke, take a special interest in him. A stranger is seen frequently near the town, the school, and the poor farm, and the truth about Jip's past is finally revealed when the teacher tells him that the stranger is really a slave catcher, out to earn bounty money. A fast-paced ending resolves the serious conflict while teaching an astounding lesson about the seriousness of the slave trade in the 1850s. This book is loosely connected to Paterson's 1991 tale, *Lyddie*, but this isn't revealed until the ending.

Silverstein, Shel. **Falling Up**. Shel Silverstein writes in the same vein as *Where the Sidewalk Ends* and *A Light in the Attic*, and delights us again with his wacky poetry. *See* POETRY.

Snyder, Zilpha Keatley. **The Gypsy Game**. New York: Delacorte Press, 1997. 217p. $15.95. ISBN 0-385-32266-6.
> The Egypt game was fun, but it's time for a change, so the same group of kids—April, Melanie, Toby, Ken, Elizabeth, and Marshall—decide to switch from imaginary scenarios about Egypt to the Gypsies. As in Zilpha Snyder's 1976 book, *The Egypt Game,* the children go to the library to collect information so that their games can be as authentic as possible. Toby adds a new twist by bringing actual Gypsy clothing, jewelry, and other artifacts that once belonged to family members—real Gypsies. The kids are now in the sixth grade, except for little Marshall, Melanie's four-year-old brother, and they know each other well. Therefore, it's

shocking when Toby disappears—possibly having been kidnapped—and what began as a game about Gypsies turns into a mystery, with the kids putting information together in their search for their friend. As it turns out, Toby has actually run away after a misunderstanding with his father, but while he is gone, he learns about being homeless and what life on the streets is like. When he's finally talked into coming home, the friends decide to turn their efforts from imaginary games to helping homeless people. Anyone who enjoyed *The Egypt Game* will find it fascinating to watch the same children grow up and begin to see the world differently. The previous book does not have to be read first to enjoy this book, but some references will make more sense if the first one has been read.

Spinelli, Jerry. **The Library Card**. New York: Scholastic Press, 1997. 148p. $15.95. ISBN 0-590-46731-X.

People who are hooked on libraries and the treasures they hold know and understand its wonder. In this book, Jerry Spinelli presents four stories about young adults—three of whom are unlikely candidates as library lovers and one who loves libraries but no longer has access to one. Each young person is offbeat and troubled in some way. A blank blue card representing a library card comes into the lives of each, and changes the way the four think and behave. Each story is a bit wacky and unusual—in true Spinelli style—which adds to the fun and mystique.

Staples, Suzanne. **Dangerous Skies**. New York: Farrar, Straus & Giroux, 1996. 231p. $16.00. ISBN 0-374-31694-5.

Buck, a White boy, and Tunes, a Black girl, have grown up together on the Chesapeake Bay and never regarded each other's skin color. Their friendship is severely tested when a neighbor's body is discovered in the bay and Tunes is suspected of committing the murder. Told in the dialogue of watermen and farmers of this region, the reader experiences life there, complete with the people's racial attitudes. Even though Buck and Tunes's families have been close for generations, they don't stand by each other during this crisis. But Buck refuses to give up, and the truth is finally revealed—with odd results. Buck tells the story years later as a young adult reflecting on the hypocrisy, bigotry, and double standard of a culture where justice is not truly equal. Suzanne Staples's use of language, dialogue, and description is outstanding, making this an exciting, and a thought-provoking work with many unexpected twists and turns.

Twain, Mark. **The Adventures of Tom Sawyer**. Illus. Claude Lapointe. New York: Viking Press, 1996. 284p. (The Whole Story Series). $23.99. ISBN 0-670-86984-8.

This is certainly not a new book, but this edition is definitely worth mentioning. It's part of a series designed to make the classics appealing and enticing to young audiences. The text is unabridged, but what sets this apart from other editions is hundreds of extended captions on the sides of the pages that give explanations about the history, geography, culture, and social customs of the time. The pages are filled with color and black-and-white drawings, sketches, photographs, maps, diagrams, and paintings that add interest and help to explain the text. High-quality paper is used, which adds to the wonderful feel of the book. *The Adventures of Tom Sawyer*, first published in 1876, is always a treat, but with all the additional trappings, this edition is a first-class product. Other books in this series are *Around the World in Eighty Days, The Call of the Wild, Heidi, The Jungle Book,* and *Treasure Island.*

Wynne Jones, Tim. **The Maestro**. New York: Orchard, 1996. 231p. $16.95. ISBN 0-531-09544-4(trade), 0-531-08894-4 (lib. bdg.).

Burl Crow, a Native American, runs away from home to escape his abusive father and drug-addicted mother. He ends up at a remote lake in the rustic cabin of a famous Canadian composer who is attempting to work in isolation from city life. They form a strong bond, and for the first time in his life Burl feels good about himself and worthwhile. After the death of the Maestro, Burl's nickname for the composer, Burl is encouraged to lay claim to the cabin. His father eventually discovers his "find" and manages to ruin yet another part of Burl's life. This book is a tribute to human resourcefulness and endurance.

Chapter 6

HIGH INTEREST—
LOW READING LEVEL

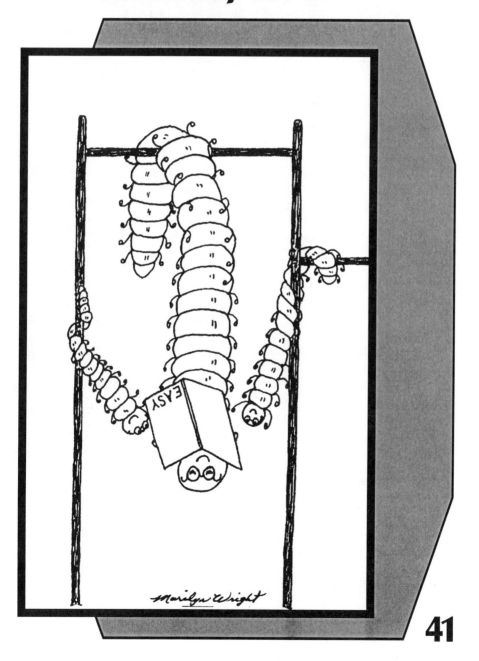

Finding books written on a low reading level yet of interest to older students is a real challenge to educators and parents. Many low-reading-level students are reluctant to read because everything of interest to them is too difficult, which takes the fun out of reading. This section includes books written on a second- to sixth-grade reading level but of high interest to preteens and teenagers. Most of the selections include action and suspense and are fairly short. These tried-and-true titles have been given to students and read and enjoyed with success.

Avi. **The Fighting Ground**. Thirteen-year-old Jonathan runs off to join the Revolutionary War and during a period of 24 hours learns the realities of war. The chapters are time periods, told by the minutes of the day. *See* UNIQUE PRESENTATIONS.

———. **Wolf Rider: A Tale of Terror**. New York: Bradbury Press, 1986. 202p. $15.00. ISBN 0-02-707760-8, 0-02-041511-7pa.
> The caller, who calls himself Zeke, claims to have killed Nina. Andy doesn't have a clue what the man is talking about, but he can't forget the conversation. He goes against the advice of his father, a university professor, and tracks down Nina, a college student, who thinks he's a crackpot and insists he leave her alone. As his investigation goes on, Andy becomes convinced that a murder is about to take place and that he is the only one who can prevent it, so he persists in his dangerous investigation. It turns out Zeke is a professor who works with Andy's father, and an exciting car-chase scene brings the mystery to a climax, with Zeke going over a drop-off and Andy becoming a hero. Showing reluctant readers the first page of the book, which contains the telephone conversation, usually hooks them. This book will not stay on the shelf once students have discovered it. It makes a terrific read aloud.

Bauer, Marion Dane. **On My Honor**. New York: Clarion Books, 1986. 90p. $11.95. ISBN 0-89919-439-7, 0-440-46633-4pa.
> Best friends all their lives, Joel and Tony spend every day together in the summer. They decide to take a bicycle trip out of town to a local park and convince their parents they'll be responsible and not go near the dangerous Vermillion River. Tony, always the daring one, talks Joel into stopping at the river and then talks Joel into swimming in the river,

even though Tony is not a good swimmer. Tony attempts to cross the river but doesn't make it, and after frantically trying to find his friend, Joel gives up the search and goes home. He locks himself in his room and tries to make reality go away, but he continues to smell the stench of the river on him no matter how long he showers. Eventually he has to admit the truth to his father and to Tony's parents, which is extremely difficult. This very short novel is about making choices and then having to live with those choices. This is an excellent book for reluctant readers because of its length, the reading level, and the lessons presented. It also makes an excellent read aloud.

Bennett, Jay. **Sing Me a Death Song**. Jason's mother is on death row, about to be executed. He is convinced she is innocent and only has a few days to prove it. This is fast paced with short chapters and easy-to-read text. *See* READ ALOUDS.

Bradley, Steve. **The Candy Man**. Belmont, CA: Fearon/Janus/Quercus, 1979. 60p. (The Pacesetter Bestsellers). $12.00. ISBN 0-8224-5265-X.
　　　　While on a flight to New York City, Peg Johnson meets Mr. Baxter, a somewhat confused traveler who seems possessive of his carry-on bag and has the nervous habit of pulling candy out of his pocket every few minutes. Upon arrival in New York the Candy Man acts even more suspicious and offers to hold Peg's coat if she'll get him a glass of water. He returns her coat to her but doesn't drink the water. She arrives at her brother's apartment, but during the night a stranger enters the apartment, demanding a statue that Peg knows nothing about. After he's driven away, she discovers a little statue tucked into her coat, obviously put there by the Candy Man. Peg and her brother decide to take it to the police, which begins a cat-and-mouse chase scene throughout New York City, with Mr. Baxter pursuing them. It turns out the statue is filled with heroin and it had been planted on Peg. She and her brother finally win the pursuit, with Mr. Baxter falling off a rooftop. This short book is action packed and suspenseful yet easy to read, making it perfect for reluctant readers. This is part of a series that includes four sets of books; Bestsellers I, Bestsellers II, Bestsellers III, and Bestsellers IV. Each set contains 10 titles of short, easy-to-read books. They are printed in paperback, but hardcovers are available through Perma-Bound.

―――. **The Sure Thing**. Belmont, CA: Fearon/Janus/Quercus, 1985. 26p. (Fastpack Sports Books). $10.00. ISBN 0-8224-6497-7.
　　　　Carmen Solar, an up-and-coming jockey, finally has the opportunity to ride in a big race and is ecstatic about it until Mr. Carillo, the owner of Fast Dancer, tries to persuade her with money to throw the race and allow Fast Dancer to win rather than her horse, Whirlwind. She refuses to be swayed by money and rides Whirlwind to victory. Mr. Carillo then admits he put his money on Whirlwind because he had the feeling she would refuse to throw the race and would ride her hardest to win. This book is small, well written, and fast paced with a good story line and is written

on a low reading level. This is part of a series of short, easy-to-read books written on a low level but with high interest. They can be used successfully with reluctant readers, English-as-a-second-language students, and special-education students. They are issued in paperback, but are available from Perma-Bound in hardcover. Other titles in this series include *Claire, The Comeback, Game Day, The Kid with the Left Hook, Marathon, Markers, Redmond's Shot, The Rookie,* and *Turk.*

Bunting, Eve. **Someone Is Hiding on Alcatraz Island**. New York: Clarion Books, 1984. 136p. $12.50. ISBN 0-89919-219-X, 0-425-10294-7pa.

Danny Sullivan is running for his life through the hills of San Francisco near Fisherman's Wharf with four ruthless Outlaw gang members—Cowboy, Maxie, Priest, and Jelly Bean—in hot pursuit. Danny decides to hop onto a tour boat headed for Alcatraz Island to escape the gang members. The Outlaws take the next boat, so they all end up on the little island, with Danny in grave danger and with no place to go. The plot thickens when all the boats for that day leave, and they are destined to spend the night on Alcatraz. A young, attractive ranger, Biddy Jarvis, is there at night also, unaware of the danger. The Outlaws capture Biddy and Danny and lock them in old prison cells. Danny's escape and how he handles the Outlaws against all odds make this an exciting book, with new twists and adventures on every page. This is a real page-turner written on a fifth-grade reading level. It makes an exciting read aloud because of the fast pace and action.

Byars, Betsy. **The 18th Emergency**. Illus. Robert Grossman. New York: Viking, 1973. 126p. $10.00. ISBN 0-14-031451-2, 0-590-44578-2pa.

Mouse's real name is Benjie, but because he's little, the name Mouse has stuck. He and his close friend, Ezzie, have put together a list of 17 ways to survive life's important emergencies, such as Emergency Three, which tells what to do if you are charged by an enraged bull. Mouse has an annoying habit of labeling things. If his shoe has a hole in it, he feels compelled to write *air vent* and draw an arrow to the hole. Marv Hammerman is the school bully, someone Mouse needs to stay away from. However, one day his compulsion to label things finds him writing Hammerman's name on the teacher's chart next to the picture of Neanderthal man. Now Emergency 18 is how to escape being beaten to a pulp by Hammerman. Mouse and Ezzie devise many different plans, but there is no escaping the bully and in the end Mouse has to take his licks. Mouse and Ezzie's antics are humorous, and their wild imaginations come up with many hilarious ideas. This is an easy-to-read, funny book that keeps the reader's interest.

DeFelice, Cynthia. **Weasel**. An evil man, Weasel, hunts people to kill for the sport of it in Ohio in 1839. He captures Nathan and Molly's father, but Ezra, a shaggy speechless man leads the children to their father.

This exciting, fast-paced book is short and easy to read, and it coordinates well with discussions of westward expansion. *See* READ ALOUDS.

Gardiner, John Reynolds. **Stone Fox**. Illus. Marcia Sewell. New York: Thomas Y. Crowell, 1980. 85p. $15.00. ISBN 0-690-03984-0, 0-440-84103-8.

When Willie's grandfather refuses to get out of bed and seemingly has given up on life, Willie is forced to carry on running the Wyoming farm by himself. He and his beloved dog, Searchlight, harvest the entire potato crop, but Grandfather still doesn't respond. Willie learns that the state of Wyoming is about to take over the farm in payment for back taxes of $500. He is seemingly helpless to save the farm until he learns about the National Dogsled Race to be held in Jackson with a prize of $500. Searchlight is a magnificent sled dog, and they practice diligently, but Stone Fox, a legendary Indian dogsledder, enters the race and is the heavy favorite to win. Stone Fox has been winning dogsled races for years, using the proceeds to buy back land previously taken from his Shoshone tribe. Willie and Searchlight get off to a good start in the race and have a narrow lead over Stone Fox until the final few yards when Searchlight's heart gives out. Stone Fox pulls up beside Willie and Searchlight, draws a line in the snow, pulls out his rifle, and demands that no one cross the line while Willie trudges across with Searchlight in his arms. This easy-to-read book is highly emotional, fast paced, impossible to put down, and long remembered.

MacLachlan, Patricia. **Sarah, Plain and Tall**. New York: Harper & Row, 1985. 58p. $13.00. ISBN 0-06-02412-0, 0-440-84813-X.

Anna and Caleb and their father, Jacob, live on the prairie during the westward expansion. The mother has died, leaving all three very lonely. Jacob advertises in a magazine for a wife, and Sarah Wheaton, from the shores of the Atlantic Ocean in Maine, answers his letter. She agrees to come West to meet the little family and has a month to decide whether she will stay and marry the father. Caleb and Anna fall in love with her, so it's a painfully long month, waiting to see whether she will stay. Sarah loves them, but the prairie is plain, and she longs for the sounds, sights, and smells of the ocean. This tender story shows the difficulties of settling the West yet shows the human side of the brave, hard-working people involved. There is a sequel, *Skylark*, which continues the story through a drought and fire and further tests of the family. Students are attracted to this book because they equate the short length with an easy read. They discover that it is rather easy to read, but the story is enticing and beautiful, making this a lovely selection.

Marlowe, Dan J. **A Game for Fools**. Belmont, CA: Fearon/Janus/Quercus, 1984. 29p. (Fastpack Mystery Books). $9.00. ISBN 0-8224-3458-X.

It's Christmastime, and Taps Enderman decides it's time to pull off his plan to steal $20,000 from the Carstairs Manufacturing Company. As he enters the office, a secretary urges him to choose an envelope from the Christmas tree, telling him that the person with the winning number will win a large amount of money. His number is 77722, a full house. As it turns out, the company only has $8,000 available in cash, so Taps settles for that and flees, thus beginning his life on the lam. He is not pleased with his new life but feels he's done what he had to do. A few days later, while holed up in a cheap motel, he reads about the Christmas Eve drawing at Carstairs and how odd it is that the person with the winning number, 77722, hasn't claimed the $10,000 prize. This short 3-x-5-inch book is easy to read but packs a great deal into it.

Mathis, Sharon Bell. **The Hundred Penny Box**. Illus. Leo Dillon and Diane Dillon. New York: Viking, 1975. 47p. $15.00. ISBN 0-670-38787-8, 0-590-42238-3.

Aunt Dew, age 100, has come to live with Michael and his family, but she spends most of her time rocking and singing and seems to be in a dream world, which is frustrating to those caring for her. The great-great-aunt has one treasure she remembers well, and that's an old "crack-up, wacky-dacky box with a broken top." She says her "years are in that box" and calls it the hundred penny box. Michael's mother thinks it should be thrown out because it's so old and banged up, but Michael and Aunt Dew love it and spend many wonderful moments with it. As Michael counts, Aunt Dew tells him what happened in her life that year. In this way she remembers all the important events in her life along with the history of the country. This is a simply told, touching story of the special bond between an old African-American woman and her great-great-nephew. It is easy to read and short, with one main story line, making it a good choice for reluctant readers.

Paulsen, Gary. **Danger on Midnight River**. New York: Bantam Doubleday Dell Books for Young Readers, 1995. 68p. (World of Adventure Series). $3.50. ISBN 0-440-41028-2pa.

Daniel is known as the dumb kid, often teased and tormented by the other kids. On the way to summer camp, he's forced to ride with three bullies who make the trip miserable. The van driver gets lost, and the van falls into a raging river. Daniel thinks he can save himself, but if he tries to find the others, he might not make it. He makes the right decision and becomes a hero.

———. **Escape from Fire Mountain**. New York: Bantam Doubleday Dell Books for Readers, 1995. 67p. (World of Adventure Series). $3.50. ISBN 0-440-41025-8pa.

Thirteen-year-old Nikki responds to a frantic message she hears on the CB radio saying that someone is trapped along the river. She takes her canoe to search for the problem and discovers a forest fire. When she reaches the bend, she finds two small children trapped by the fire. As she tries to get them to safety, Nikki is pursued by poachers who believe she's seen too much of their illegal operation. Nikki finds herself battling the river, the forest fire, and the poachers as she tries to take the two children to safety.

————. **The Gorgon Slayer.** New York: Bantam Doubleday Dell Books for Young Readers, 1995. 51p. (World of Adventure Series). $3.50. ISBN 0-440-41041-Xpa.

> Prince Charming's Damsel in Distress Rescue Agency employs young boys to slay dragons, kill gorgons, or do whatever brave deeds need to be done. This is a wacky mixture of the days of yore with a host of mythical creatures and modern-day kids watching television, eating candy bars, and riding bicycles. This easy to read story will be enjoyed by students who are somewhat familiar with the Greek gods and mythical creatures and can understand that this is an offbeat spoof on heroism.

————. **Harris and Me: A Summer Remembered.** Gary Paulsen and his cousin, Harris, spend a summer of misadventures on Harris's farm in Minnesota. *See* READ ALOUDS.

————. **Hatchet.** A boy's plane crashes in the wilderness, and he's stranded with only a hatchet to help him survive. The reading level is fifth grade, and interest level extends through high school. *See* SCIENCE.

————. **The Legend of Red Horse Cavern.** New York: Bantam Doubleday Dell Books for Young Readers, 1994. 55p. (World of Adventure Series). $3.50. ISBN 0-440-41023-1pa.

> Will and Sarah have heard the old Apache legend many times about how Red Horse, a Native American brave who betrayed his people, was beheaded and now haunts the mountain range searching for his head. They begin to believe the legend when they explore a cave and discover a chest filled with one million dollars and bandits pursue them. They feel both the bandits and Red Horse are after them when they lose their way and all seems hopeless in the cold, dark cavern. This is an action-packed, fast-paced page-turner.

————. **Nightjohn.** A short but powerful novel about slavery and the importance of reading. *See* SOCIAL STUDIES—UNITED STATES HISTORY.

————. **Project: A Perfect World.** New York: Bantam Doubleday Dell Books for Young Readers, 1996. 74p. (World of Adventure Series). $3.99. ISBN 0-440-41026-6pa.

> Everyone in Jim's family is happy about their move to a small town in New Mexico except Jim. He finds it strange that everyone in the town dresses and acts alike and seems to do exactly what the bosses at Folsum Laboratories demand. Jim ventures off into the mountains and discovers that the lab is involved in a mind-control experiment involving his family.

————. **The Rock Jockeys**. New York: Bantam Doubleday Dell Books for Young Readers, 1995. 55p. (World of Adventure Series). $3.50. ISBN 0-440-41026-6pa.

Rick, J. D., and Spud, Rock Jockeys, are determined to climb a treacherous mountain to look for the remains of a B-17 bomber that supposedly crashed into the mountain many years before. They do find the remains of the plane, but they also discover human remains and the navigator's diary, which reveals secrets that make their climb even more dangerous.

————. **The Seventh Crystal**. New York: Bantam Doubleday Dell Books for Young Readers, 1996. 71p. (World of Adventure Series). $3.99. ISBN 0-440-41051-7.

Someone anonymously sends Jimmy the computer game, *The Seventh Crystal*. It's not often he's stumped by a computer game, but this one has him puzzled. While on an errand to the store, he and his friend, Chris, encounter two bullies who have been making life difficult for Jimmy by beating him up and taking his money. Chris and Jimmy run to escape the bullies, but the computer game comes alive. It's set in medieval times, so they encounter many evils, including swamp monsters, storms, black knights, a dragon, and giants. They eventually win the game by saving the princess, and they become friends with the bullies.

NOTE: Each title in The World of Adventure series is action filled, with teenagers (usually male) in scary, mysterious situations. Each book is written on a second- to fourth-grade reading level and is exciting and sure to please slower, reluctant, and emergent readers. Even though each title has few pages, the story is well told, and the characters are developed. Paulsen understands the need for well-written high-lows and is continuing to add to this series. They are available only in paperback.

Chapter 7
MATHEMATICS

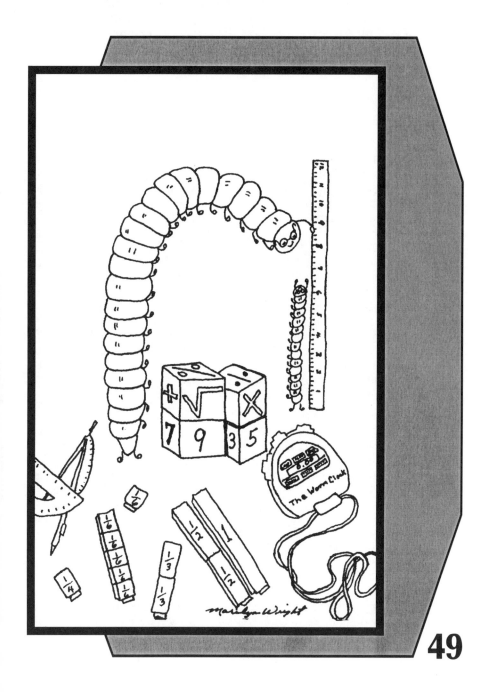

49

The true meaning of mathematics is realized when it is used for real-life situations rather than work sheets filled with computational problems. Each book in this section presents mathematics using practical applications, often to explore a specific concept. The books in this section will help teach specific concepts and add spark and fun when exploring mathematics.

Anno, Mitsumasa. **Anno's Magic Seeds**. New York: Philomel Books, 1995. Unpaged. $15.95. ISBN 0-399-22538-2.

Jack is given two magic seeds by a wizard. Each year he eats one, and it satisfies his food needs for the entire year. He plants the other seed, and it produces a plant with two new seeds. He performs the same ritual year after year until he becomes bored and decides to try something new, planting both seeds and eating other things during the year. Both plants produce two seeds each, so he eats one, plants three, and therefore, begins farming, increasing his seed output each year. At the end of each two-page spread, the reader is asked mathematical questions based on the amount of planting Jack does in a year. He marries Alice and shares his seeds with her, still ending up with excess output, so they begin to sell their seeds, which begins commerce and trade. The story is amusing, the illustrations are filled with humorous details, and mathematical and social situations are presented repeatedly. What a fun way to practice mathematical applications!

———. **Anno's Math Games II**. New York: Philomel Books, 1989. 103p. $20.00. ISBN 0-399-21615-4.

Anno is a master at presenting intriguing problems and asking the reader to figure them out. In this volume each of the five sections represents a different type of math problem, each requiring careful observation and reasoning. Two little men, Kriss and Kross, present all the action. Section 1, "The Magic Machine," uses a machine that has an opening on the left and one on the right. Items are put into one opening and come out the other end in a different form. The reader needs to figure out what caused the change and what relationship exists between the things on the left and the things on the right. Section 2, "Compare and Find Out," uses comparison to look for likenesses and differences for problem solving. Section 3, "Dots, Dots, and More Dots," shows that many dots all put together can create pictures. Kriss and Kross use a variety of methods to show that all things are just a bunch of dots assembled together, including human beings. Section 4, "Counting with

Circles" deals with symbolism in math using a variety of ways to show the relationship between a numeral and its value. In the final section, "Counting Water," Kriss and Kross measure cups of water to illustrate the metric system. Each drawing in the book is done in a light, comical manner but helps the reader with the problem presented on that page.

————. **Anno's Math Games III**. New York: Philomel Books, 1991. 103p. $12.95. ISBN 0-698-11673-9pa.

Anno has a unique perspective on mathematics and portrays his curiosity and questioning using humor and illustrations. In this volume he presents the topics of topology in Section 1, pointing out that things appear to change shape depending on what perspective is taken. Section 2 uses tangrams to explore triangles. Section 3 explores mazes and how to make them and Section 4 explores in-depth how left and right affect us. Our familiar friends Kriss and Kross do all the presenting and experimenting, moving objects around to fit the narrative. Anno inspires mathematical thinking and has fun along the way.

Anno, Mitsumasa, and Masaichiro Anno. **Anno's Mysterious Multiplying Jar**. New York: Philomel Books, 1983. 45p. $17.95. ISBN 0-399-20951-4.

Mitsumasa Anno and his son, Masaichiro Anno, use a story about a water jar and the many items in it to illustrate the mathematical idea of factorials. The beautifully illustrated story presents the mathematical problem beginning with one water jar filled with one island. On each island there are two countries, and within each country there are three mountains. On each mountain there are four kingdoms and so forth until we reach ten items. Ten factorial (10!) is then explained using text and illustrations. This is a highly useful and entertaining tool to teach the concept of factorials.

Birch, David. **The King's Chessboard**. Illus. Devis Grebu. New York: Puffin Pied Piper Books, 1988. $5.99. ISBN 0-14-054880-7pa.

This is a retelling of the classic story of the king who wants to reward a faithful servant, and the servant agrees to be paid with grains of rice with the amount doubling each day. In this version the servant agrees to be given rice each day until all 64 squares on his chessboard are filled. The king, not understanding math, believes this is a good arrangement and doesn't understand that if he doubles the amount of rice every day for 64 days, it will require more rice than is in the entire world. The servant finally approaches the king and allows him to back out of the deal. This story is the same concept presented in Demi's *One Grain of Rice: A Mathematical Folktale*, listed in this section.

Clement, Rod. **Counting on Frank**. Milwaukee, WI: Gareth Stevens Publishing, 1991. Unpaged. $18.00. ISBN 0-8368-0358-2.

The narrator is a curious fellow, questioning the simple things in life, such as if he knocked 15 peas off his plate every night for eight years, how high would the peas be stacked on the floor? When a competition is held to guess how many jelly beans are in a jar and the prize is a trip to Hawaii, he wins because he knows there are 745 jelly beans, because that's how many jelly beans fit into an average candy jar. Frank, the family dog, plays a part in each question. Each two-page spread is a hilarious situation, always dealing with an offbeat mathematics problem. The illustrations are overstated and cartoonlike. A section at the end, "Here's a Chance to Use YOUR Brain!" discusses each problem and asks additional questions. This is a how-to on having fun with math.

Cooney, Miriam P., ed. **Celebrating Women in Mathematics and Science**. Illus. Kevin Chadwick. Reston, VA: Doubleday, 1996. 223p. $22.50. ISBN 0-87353-425-5pa.

In an effort to promote women in mathematics and science, a group of teachers affiliated with Saint Mary's College, Notre Dame, Indiana, gathered information on 22 women who have contributed significantly to the development of science and mathematics throughout history. Each section consists of a few pages of excellent information, along with a woodcut depicting each woman and a bibliography of suggested readings. The collection of women begins with Hypatia and includes other well-known people such as Florence Nightingale and Elizabeth Blackwell, but also includes many lesser-known women, such as Emilie du Chatelet and Barbara McClintock. Modern-day scientists such as Dian Fossey and Jane Goodall are also included. Each section is written in an easy-to-read, inviting format and is excellent for report writing or recreational reading.

Demi. **One Grain of Rice: A Mathematical Folktale**. New York: Scholastic, 1997. Unpaged. $19.95. ISBN 0-590-93998-X.

Demi combines an old Indian tale with striking artwork to illustrate the principle of doubling and the powers of two. Years ago, a raja in India laid claim to nearly all the rice each subject grew, with the excuse of storing the rice in case of famine. A famine indeed comes and the people are starving, but the raja won't open the storehouses. Rani, a village girl, does the raja a favor and as a reward he grants her anything she wants. She asks to be given one grain of rice on the first day and then double that amount each day for 30 days. The raja thinks she's a simpleton but soon discovers that it takes many baskets and bags of rice to fulfill his promise. By the thirtieth day it requires the contents of four royal storehouses carried on 256 elephants to complete his promise. Demi illustrates this dramatically by displaying the elephants on two fold-out pages. A chart is presented at the conclusion showing how much rice was given each day and how the doubling worked. The reader is then challenged to add all the grains together to see how much rice Rani received altogether.

Geisert, Arthur. **Roman Numerals I to MM = Numerabilia Romana Uno Ad Duo Mila: Liber De Difficillimo Computando Numerum**. Boston: Houghton Mifflin, 1996. 32p. $15.95. ISBN 0-395-74519-5.

Roman numerals are described and explained with just enough text to make the concepts clear and well understood, but the illustrations using pigs are the most instructive. Roman numerals are presented along with the equivalent number of pigs engaged in all types of activities. For instance, the number L has 50 pigs climbing and playing on a large jungle gym, and the number C has 100 pigs playing on and around four teeter-totters. On every page pigs are having a marvelous time at some recreational activity normally enjoyed by children, not pigs, making this a funny book. Students will have fun examining the hilarious activities while learning what each Roman numeral means. Toward the end, the Roman numerals are listed and represented in the illustrations by various objects, such as III tractors, XI evergreen trees, XV balloons, XXVII fence posts, I seventeen sixty-six, and MMMMDCCCLXIV pigs.

Hopkins, Lee Bennett. **Marvelous Math: A Book of Poems**. Illus. Karen Barbour. New York: Simon & Schuster Books for Young Readers, 1997. 32p. $17.00. ISBN 0-689-80658-2.

Mathematics comes in many forms as seen in this collection of 16 poems about math, each touching on a different aspect of it. The title poem, "Marvelous Math," uses beautiful language to point out why mathematics is necessary. A particularly touching entry is "Math Makes Me Feel Safe," in which the narrator explains that mathematical things remain the same, bringing security. A perfect tie-in with science is "Sky," in which the poet sees decimal points, fractions, and percentages in the night sky. The full-page brilliantly colored illustrations help to make this a delightful book.

Lasky, Kathryn. **The Librarian Who Measured the Earth**. Illus. Kevin Hawkes. New York: Little, Brown, 1994. 48p. $16.95. ISBN 0-316-51526-4.

Eratosthenes was an amazing man who left his mark in literature, science, mathematics, and geography. He was born in ancient Greece but spent most of his life in Alexandria, where he became the chief librarian at the renowned Alexandria Library. His need to question and find answers to those questions caused him to make outstanding discoveries. His best-known discovery was to determine the circumference of the Earth using angles and shadows cast by the sun at noon on June 21. His accomplishments are described in a fascinating manner in a book that can easily fit into mathematics, science, social studies, and English curricula. The Afterword gives a summary of important discoveries throughout time, many of them using Eratosthenes' work as their basis.

Mori, Tuyosi. **Socrates and the Three Little Pigs**. Illus. Mitsumasa Anno. New York: Philomel Books, 1986. 44p. $13.95. ISBN 0-399-21310-4.

Socrates the wolf is a thinker, and his friend Pythagoras the frog is a mathematician. Socrates's wife, Xanthippe, is hungry and grumpy and would like one of the three little pigs that live in the meadow for her dinner. Socrates would be happy to catch one for her, but he doesn't know which of the five houses to go to for a pig. He and Pythagoras begin to use mathematical concepts to determine the odds of finding one pig alone in one of the houses, making it easy prey. They study the patterns and combinations, called combinatorics or combinatorial analysis, to answer their problem. Little boxes with pictures of happy little pigs are drawn in many different arrangements, with text describing the entire procedure. The reader is led through the process by examining each set of pictures and following the text. Socrates and his friend come up with hundreds of variables and finally make a determination about the arrangement of the pigs. However, as they look at the cute little happy pigs, they decide the best solution of all is to be friends with them and play together rather than to eat them. A detailed description of the mathematical process used to determine the solution is given at the end of the book. This is a great tool to use when studying patterns or when simply having fun with math.

Nozaki, Akihiro. **Anno's Hat Tricks**. Illus. Mitsumasa Anno. New York: Philomel Books, 1985. 44p. $13.95. ISBN 0-399-21212-4.

Logical thinking and mathematical problem-solving are introduced with the help of two children, Tom and Hannah, while a third person, Shadowchild, asks the questions. Tom and Hannah are made to guess the color of the hats on their heads. The puzzles begin simply, and the questions asked are easy to answer. Two red hats and one white hat are used to help illustrate the problems. However, as the book continues, five hats are used—three red and two white—causing a higher level of difficulty in the puzzles, and higher-level thinking skills are necessary to solve the problems. Questions are asked in a clever manner, and the illustrator shows the situation in a simple yet clever way. A section at the back of the book explains the binary logic process and answers some of the problems. The ideas presented are fun for "openers" in math class, and puzzle lovers will pour over this book.

Reimer, Luetta, and Wilbert Reimer. **Mathematicians Are People, Too: Stories from the Lives of Great Mathematicians**. Palo Alto, CA: Dale Seymour Publications, 1990. 143p. $13.00. ISBN 0-86651-509-7pa.

Mathematics is a human endeavor, and there is often a fascinating story behind important mathematical discoveries. The purpose of this book is to show that mathematics is intriguing and a part of our heritage and that it has fascinated people throughout time. It accomplishes this by presenting biographies of 15 important mathematicians, including Thales, Pythagoras, Archimedes, Hypatia, John Napier, Galileo, Pascal, Sir Isaac Newton, Leonhard Euler, Joseph Lagrange, Sophie St. Germain,

Carl Gauss, Evariste Galois, Amalie Noether, and Arinivasa Ramanujan. More than 100 anecdotes and stories are included, each designed to stimulate interest in mathematics. The topics of problem solving, geometry, number system and theory, algebra, computation and estimation, probability and statistics, women in mathematics, measurement, and mathematical symbols are presented through storytelling. The biographies are written in a light, readable manner, making it an excellent read aloud for math. A resource list of books on the history of mathematics and a detailed glossary help to make this a highly useful book.

Sachar, Louis. **More Sideways Arithmetic from Wayside School**. New York: Scholastic, 1994. 94p. $2.95. ISBN 0-590-47762-5.

Fifty-eight seemingly random problems arranged into 14 sections are presented in a silly scenario, but when the reader takes a closer look, they make sense, and the problems can be answered. Students who know Louis Sachar from his fiction novels know he's slightly crazy, so it's no surprise that his scenarios are nutty and fun filled. The problems presented in this volume can be used as openers or as a part of a regular math lesson. The notes and clues given in the back help to explain the procedures and strategies needed to solve these problems, and an answer section is given. This is a sequel to the equally zany *Sideways Arithmetic from Wayside School*.

Sandburg, Carl. **Arithmetic: Illustrated as an Anamorphic Adventure by Ted Rand**. Illus. Ted Rand. New York: Harcourt Brace Jovanovich, 1993. 32p. $15.95. ISBN 0-15-203865-5.

In 1933, Carl Sandburg published his famous "Arithmetic" poem in which he talks about numbers and all the fun things you can do with them. Ted Rand has added his own kind of fun to the poem by using anamorphic images to stretch or condense, which then distort the picture. However, if the Mylar sheet included with the book is wrapped around a cylindrical can, or if you close one eye and look at the illustrations from the vantage point of the red arrow in each picture, the images will appear correct and normal. An explanation of anamorphic is given at the end of the book, along with instructions on how to make anamorphic drawings. This book will help make math enjoyable both by reading the poem and by constructing anamorphic drawings using measurement and other mathematics.

Schwartz, David M. **How Much Is a Million?** Illus. Steven Kellogg. New York: Lothrop, 1985. 40p. $18.50. ISBN 0-688-04050-0, 0-590-43614-7pa.

It's difficult to imagine how big 1 million really is, but Schwartz, along with Steven Kellogg's active drawings, vividly illustrates, in a variety of ways, just what it would take to make a million. If you had 1 million goldfish, it would take a fishbowl large enough to hold a whale. Counting to 1 million would take 23 days. Using equally fun and vivid examples, they describe how much it takes to make a billion and then a trillion. The text is simple and easy to read. The illustrations depict young children, but the concepts discussed are appropriate for all ages. The author adds notes at the end, discussing the mathematical concepts presented in the book.

————. **If You Made a Million**. Illus. Steven Kellogg. New York: Lothrop, 1989. 40p. $18.50. ISBN 0-688-07018-3, 0-590-43608-2pa.

Money and banking are relevant to every person's life, but students often have a difficult time understanding the concepts involved. Schwartz takes one single penny and transforms it into 1 million dollars by presenting a wild and crazy story along with hilarious Steven Kellogg illustrations. Along the way we learn about money denominations, banking, loans and interest, real estate, income tax, and just exactly what 1 million means. The author's notes at the end of the book further explain the concepts discussed in the text and give historical background as well as mathematical explanations.

Scieszka, Jon, and Lane Smith. **Math Curse**. New York: Penguin Books, 1995. 20p. $18.00. ISBN 0-670-86194-4.

Have you ever had students question why they're asked to do math? If so, this book will answer that question. Scieszka and Lane present a real-life situation involving math, make it hilariously funny, and add wild, splashy illustrations, creating the perfect recipe for reasons to "do math." The person telling the story gets up at 7:15 A.M., takes 10 minutes to dress, 15 minutes to eat breakfast, and one minute to brush his teeth; he realizes he now has math problems. Will he make his 8:00 bus? How many minutes are in one hour, and how many teeth are in one mouth? Throughout the day he encounters one math problem after the next, including measuring problems in social studies, compound-word problems in English, baseball averages in physical education and ancient Mayan numerals in art. Each oversize two-page spread presents a new situation, one funnier than the next.

Smoothey, Marion. **Angles**. Illus. Ted Evans. New York: Marshall Cavendish, 1993. 64p. (Let's Investigate). $17.00. ISBN 1-85435-466-3, 1-85435-463-9 (set).

————. **Area and Volume**. Illus. Ted Evans. New York: Marshall Cavendish, 1993. 64p. (Let's Investigate). $17.00. ISBN 1-85435-460-4, 1-85435-455-8 (set).

————. **Circles**. Illus. Ted Evans. New York: Marshall Cavendish, 1993. 64p. (Let's Investigate). $17.00. ISBN 1-85435-456-6, 1-85435-455-8 (set).

―――. **Number Patterns**. Illus. Ted Evans. New York: Marshall Cavendish, 1993. 64p. (Let's Investigate). $17.00. ISBN 1-85435-458-2, 1-85435-455-8 (set).

―――. **Numbers**. Illus. Ted Evans. New York: Marshall Cavendish, 1993. 64p. (Let's Investigate). $17.00. ISBN 1-85435-457-4, 1-85435-455-8 (set).

―――. **Quadrilaterals**. Illus. Ted Evans. New York: Marshall Cavendish, 1993. 64p. (Let's Investigate). $17.00. ISBN 1-85435-459-0, 1-85435-455-8 (set).

―――. **Statistics**. Illus. Ted Evans. New York: Marshall Cavendish, 1993. 64p. (Let's Investigate). $17.00. ISBN 5435-468-X, 1-85435-463-9 (set).

―――. **Triangles**. Illus. Ted Evans. New York: Marshall Cavendish, 1993. 64p. (Let's Investigate). $17.00. ISBN 1-85435-461-2, 1-85435-455-8 (set).

Each volume in this useful series deals with only the subject named in the title. Because each topic is separate, it is explored and explained thoroughly rather than with just a cursory glance, which is often the case when too much information is put into one volume. Each main topic is divided into several subtopics and clearly explained with text and illustrations. Students interested in math ideas will enjoy pondering the material and trying out the activities. Teachers will find this set a valuable teaching tool when presenting specific topics. Each volume contains a glossary, an answer section, and an index.

Tahan, Malba. **The Man Who Counted: A Collection of Mathematical Adventures**. Trans. Leslie Clark and Alastair Reid, illus. Patricia Reid Baquero. New York: W. W. Norton, 1993. 244p. $14.00. ISBN 0-393-30934-7pa.

In each short story, Beremiz Samir, from Persia, who has met up with another traveler, Hanak Tade Maia, tells a story and solves a mystery by using mathematics. The two men travel together, and as they meet new situations, Beremiz is able to solve perplexing problems by using logical thinking skills. He has never had any formal mathematical training, so each problem is solved and explained in a simple-to-understand manner. Beremiz does the problem solving, and Hanak does the storytelling, describing life in the Middle East as they wander along. Much is learned about the history and customs of the area as they travel and talk. Each section is only two to six pages long, lending itself well to oral reading, both in math and social studies.

Tompert, Ann. **Grandfather Tang's Story: A Tale Told with Tangrams**. Illus. Robert Andrew Parker. New York: Crown, 1990. 32p. $16.00. ISBN 0-517-57487-X (trade), 0-517-57272-9 (lib. bdg.).

In this old Chinese folktale Grandfather Tang uses tangrams to tell his granddaughter, Little Soo, a story about two foxes who change themselves into different shapes. Using the seven standard tangram pieces, Grandfather Tang makes a fox, a rabbit, a dog, a squirrel, a hawk, a turtle, a crocodile, a goldfish, a goose, a lion and an old man, a young girl, and a tree. As he tells the story, he rearranges the pieces to fit whichever animal or person he's describing. A picture of each figure is given, so students can reproduce what Grandfather Tang did. Using these tangrams students can investigate geometrical concepts and retell or invent their own stories.

MULTICULTURAL

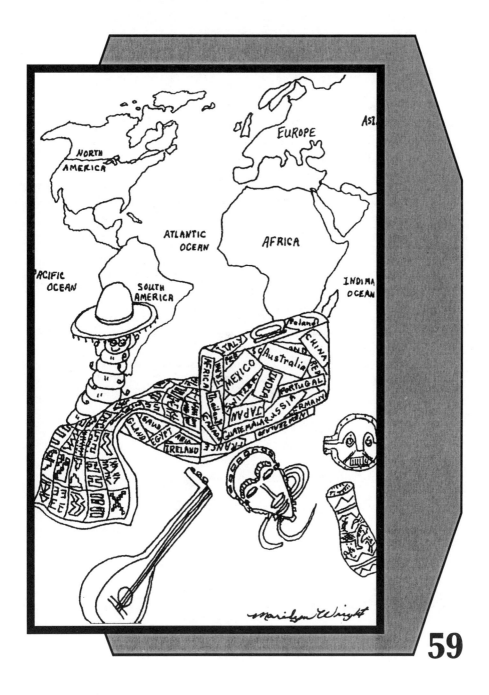

59

Countries and cultures from around the world are celebrated through the beautiful children's literature presented in this section. Some of the most outstanding literature and artwork recently has been in works in this area that help readers learn about and celebrate diversity.

Ada, Alma Flor. **Gathering the Sun: An Alphabet in Spanish and English**. Trans. Rosa Zubizarreta, illus. Simón Silva. New York: Lothrop, Lee & Shepard, 1997. Unpaged. $16.00. ISBN 0-688-1303-5 (trade), 0-688-13904-3 (lib. bdg.).
This is one of the most richly colored, beautiful, and exciting dual-language books on the market. Each page is filled with vibrant illustrations beautifully describing the poem on that page. This collection of poetry, one for each letter of the Spanish alphabet, is about working in the fields and the beauty and bounty of nature. Each poem is written in Spanish along with the English translation. It begins with a poem "Arboles," which describes the many fruit trees important to farmworkers. B is for betabel, or beet, and a special tribute is made to César Chavez for the letter C. A magnificent full-page painting of Chavez along with the United Farm Worker's symbol surrounds the poem describing his important work. Each poem celebrates the pride, family, friends, history, and heritage of the farmworkers and the contributions they have made and continue to make to society. The author and the illustrator feel strongly about their heritage and have produced an outstanding tribute to it. This is an excellent example of Mexican-American art.

Bateson-Hill, Margaret. **Lao Lao of Dragon Mountain**. Chinese text Manyee Wan, illus. Francesca Pelizzoli, paper cuts Sha-Liu Qu. A Chinese folktale uses paper cuts to help tell the story. The Chinese translation is included. See FINE ARTS.

Bray, Rosemary. **Martin Luther King**. Illus. Malcah Zeldis. This extended-text picture book is a moving and inspiring biography of Martin Luther King Jr. See BIOGRAPHIES.

Bunting, Eve. **Going Home**. Illus. David Diaz. New York: Harper-Collins, 1996. 32p. $15.00. ISBN 0-06-026296-6 (trade), 0-06-026297-4 (lib. bdg.).

Mama and Papa often talk about "going home," but the children are confused. Home to them is the farm on which their parents work in Texas, so they're unclear about their parents' idea of home. At Christmastime the family piles into their car, and they travel for four days to get to La Perla, Mexico, the town where Mama and Papa grew up. The children have trouble understanding why they had to make the trip but soon realize that their parents love this place and all their relatives and left it because they wanted their children to have more opportunities. Their parents' love for their children is so strong they are willing to sacrifice everything for them. This is a powerful, impressive work expressing the desires of many immigrant families.

Carlson, Lori M., ed. **Cool Salsa: Bilingual Poems on Growing Up Latino in the United States**. Intro. Oscar Hijuelos. New York: Henry Holt, 1994. 123p. $14.95. ISBN 0-8050-3135-9.

Each of the poems in this collection was written by a Latino living in the United States and captures the flavor of what it's like to live in two cultures, speak two languages, trying to belong to both worlds. Each poem deals with a different aspect of living in two cultures. Some of the poems are fiery, some sad, while others celebrate their heritage. But each has a story to tell and does it well. Each poem is written in both Spanish and English, which adds to the meaning and usefulness of the collection.

Cha, Dia. **Dia's Story Cloth: The Hmong People's Journey of Freedom**. Stitched by Chue and Nhia Thad Cha. New York: Lee and Low Books, 1996. 24p. $14.95; ISBN 1-880000-34-2.

Throughout time cultures have passed stories on to future generations. The Hmongs in this book have chosen to tell their story of flight and immigration through a story cloth, an embroidered hanging that beautifully depicts their history. This is a unique work, excellent for sharing with an entire class when discussing other cultures, storytelling, or art. This book is a "must" for teachers with Hmong children in their classes.

Choi, Sook Nyul. **Gathering of Pearls**. Boston: Houghton Mifflin, 1994. 163p. $13.95. ISBN 0-395-67437-9.

In this third novel Sookan Bak, the brave and determined girl who survived the Korean War in *Year of Impossible Goodbyes* and the reconstruction of their lives in *Echoes of the White Giraffe* has won a scholarship to a college in the United States and begins a new chapter in her life. Her English is halting, but she is determined to excel in college because she wants to make her family in Korea proud of her. She has little money, so she works several jobs, and even though her English is poor, she insists on taking a full load of heavy academic classes. She makes friends easily, but she has little time to socialize because of her heavy workload. However, her biggest struggle is trying to fit into American ways and still follow the customs of her Korean upbringing. She does a remarkable job of tying the two cultures together and even helps her two best friends to better understand their parents by sharing some of the wisdom from the Korean culture. This series is autobiographical because the events described are based on the author's own experiences. Much can be learned from this courageous and remarkable woman.

Cisneros, Sandra. **The House on Mango Street**. New York: Vintage Contemporaries, 1984. 110p. $9.00. ISBN 0-679-73477-5.
    The life story of Esperanza Cordero, a young Mexican-American woman, is told through a series of vignettes describing her life in the inner city of Chicago. She tells about her family, the crowded living conditions, her run-down neighborhood, and life around her. She is determined not to continue her life with low expectations but to empower herself with determination and education. She examines the people in her life and makes a serious and conscious effort to better herself. This is a brave work from a Mexican-American woman stepping out of the mold to go against the norm. The stories are short and told just the way Esperanza thinks. This book is a powerful tool to use with students who need a positive role model.

Coburn, Jewell Reinhart, with Tzexa Cherta Lee. **Jouanah: A Hmong Cinderella**. Illus. Anne Sibley O'Brien. A Hmong version of Cinderella. *See* MYTHS, FOLKTALES, AND LEGENDS.

Cumpián, Carlos. **Latino Rainbow: Poems About Latino Americans**. Illus. Richard Leonard. Chicago: Childrens Press, 1994. 47p. $16.00. ISBN 0-516-05153-9.
    With the growing numbers of Latino children in our schools, this book can fill many needs. It can help Latino children to understand those in their culture who have done important work, and it can help non-Latinos to better understand this culture. This is a collection of 20 poems that give biographies of Americans of Latino heritage who have contributed to American society. The poetry is written in free verse and flows like a story. For better understanding of the poems, the author encourages the reader to read the poems out loud while standing up. Fifteen poems are about specific individuals or families: Louis Agassiz Fuertes, Bernardo Vega, the Ronstadt family, Luis Alvarez, Dr. Hector Garcia, Ritchie Valens, Tito Puente, César Chavez, Roberto Clemente, Carlos Cortez, Joan Baez, Reies López Tijerina, Antonia Coelho Novello, Henry Cisneros, and Ellen Ochoa. The other five are about groups or causes, such as the California Rancheros, the Treaty of Guadalupe Hidalgo, the Cuban refugees, the Neorican Poets, and the Central American refugees. The brightly colored illustrations fit the text well and help to tell the stories.

Garland, Sherry. **Shadow of the Dragon**. New York: Harcourt Brace, 1993. 314p. $10.95. ISBN 0-15-273530-5, 0-15-273532-1pa.

> The Vo family managed to escape Vietnam and come to the United States in hope of a good life, especially for their children. However, as in many immigrant families, the children have a difficult time living in the new world yet keeping the old customs. Danny Vo's parents work long hours, expecting the children to do well in school and work hard, but their daughter, Kim, is becoming disobedient, wearing clothes that are unacceptable to the parents and grandmother. Danny also sees his cousin, Sang Le, get involved with a dangerous Vietnamese gang, the Cobras, and he's helpless to make Sang Le understand that this is not the correct path to follow. At the same time, Danny begins dating a White girl, Tiffany, whose brother is a White supremacist skinhead vehemently opposed to Danny dating his sister. This mixture and clashing of cultures comes to a head when the White supremacists mistake Sang Le for Danny and kill Sang Le. Danny reaches far back into his Vietnamese culture to find solace and solutions to the conflicts.

Hamilton, Virginia. **Her Stories: African American Folktales, Fairy Tales, and True Tales**. Illus. Leo Dillon and Diane Dillon. This rich, colorful collection of animal tales, fairy tales, tales of the supernatural, folkways, and legends and true tales all involve Black women. *See* MYTHS, FOLKTALES, AND LEGENDS.

Hicyilmaz, Gaye. **Against the Storm**. Boston: Little, Brown, 1990. 200p. $14.95. ISBN 0-316-36078-3.

> Mehmet's family dreams of more than just subsisting in the countryside living from hand to mouth. His father packs everyone up, abandoning their small home, and they head for the big city, Ankara, Turkey. The family find themselves in much poorer housing with little to eat and at the mercy of their rich, obnoxious, and scheming uncle. Mehmet is no longer able to go to school because the family cannot afford it, so he spends his time roaming the streets, learning a new, harsher way of life. This is an important work because it aptly portrays the plight of the poor in third-world countries. The dream of making life easier and better often fades rather than prospers when people move to a city. Harsh reality is shown by the plight of several friends who are injured or fall prey to evildoing because of their economic status. The adults, taken out of their familiar countryside, are easy prey in their new setting and are unable to help the children. It does end on a hopeful note, however, as Mehmet heads back to the countryside to try to regain what he once had. A useful glossary of terms is included.

Hudson, Wade. **Pass It On: African-American Poetry for Children**. Illus. Floyd Cooper. Nineteen poems by 14 African-American poets represent a wide variety of poetry about the African-American experience. *See* POETRY.

Kidd, Diana. **Onion Tears**. Illus. Lucy Montgomery. New York: Orchard, 1989. 62p. $12.95. ISBN 0-531-05870-0, 0-531-08470-1 (lib. bdg.).

The Vietnam War took its toll on many people in many ways. Nam-Huong, a young Vietnamese girl, is in America, living with Auntie, a woman who takes in foster Vietnamese children. Nam-Huong has been so traumatized by the war that she no longer speaks to anyone in any language. She goes to school, where students poke fun at her because of the way she looks and the type of food she eats and because she doesn't speak. Nam-Huong tells the story of her everyday life within the regular text, but her deep, inner thoughts about Vietnam and the war are told to her animal friends she had in Vietnam: a canary, a duck, and a buffalo. She tells the animals how sad she is and how desperately she needs to know the whereabouts of her parents and other family members. In her talks with the animals, she chronicles the flight from Vietnam, ending with getting on a boat with her grandfather and being on the water a long time. In the regular text, Nam-Huong tells about the harassment at school as it worsens and how her only friend is her teacher, Miss Lily. When Miss Lily becomes ill, Nam-Huong goes to her house to care for her dog, Samson. One day Samson runs into the water and she's fearful he will drown. This brings back a flood of emotion, reminding Nam-Huong of the boat ride and her grandfather's death while on the boat. Suddenly she's calling out loud to Samson and to her parents, breaking her long silence. Miss Lily finds her, and Nam-Huong tells Miss Lily her sad story, which frees her and allows her to continue talking. School becomes more enjoyable for Nam-Huong, and the other children stop their teasing and include her as their real friend. This short, but moving story says much in just a few pages. It portrays the horrors of war and the toll it takes.

Kimmel, Eric A. **The Three Princes: A Tale from the Middle East**. A Middle Eastern folktale about a princess trying to choose a husband. *See* MYTHS, FOLKTALES, AND LEGENDS.

Lankford, Mary. **Hopscotch Around the World**. By describing how hopscotch is played around the world, we can see similarities among cultures. *See* SPORTS AND GAMES.

———. **Jacks Around the World**. The game of jacks is played all over the world, each country using slightly different rules and equipment, but the basic game is similar. *See* SPORTS AND GAMES.

Lewin, Ted. **Market!** New York: Lothrop, Lee & Shepard, 1996. 48p. $16.00. ISBN 0-688-12161-6 (trade), 0-688-12162-4 (lib. bdg.).

Markets are the backbone of all societies, whether housed in a large mall or spread out under tents and canopies. In Ted Lewin's travels he researched marketplaces and recorded their wonders and uniqueness in this work. Each page is filled with colorful, detailed drawings clearly depicting the wares and the people of each market. Lewin takes the reader to Ecuador, Nepal, Ireland, Uganda, New York City, and Morocco. Lewin's work shows the many similarities of cultures all around the world.

Martinez, Victor. **Parrot in the Oven: Mi Vida/A Novel**. New York: HarperCollins, 1996. 216p. $14.95. ISBN 0-06-026704-6 (trade), 0-06-026706-2 (lib. bdg.).

In this semiautobiographical work, Victor Martinez presents what it was like to grow up in the Central Valley of California as a poor Mexican-American. This collection of short stories portrays the culture, the foods, and the lifestyle of his family and what it was like to be the one in the family who wanted to succeed and become more useful to society than his alcoholic father and passive mother. He wanted to learn and continue his education, but it was an uphill struggle. In a straightforward manner, each story describes another aspect of his life, from picking chilies in the field to gang life to reverence for his grandmother. This is an excellent read aloud because of the short-story format, its descriptive language, and the subject matter.

Mathis, Sharon Bell. **The Hundred Penny Box**. Illus. Leo Dillon and Diane Dillon. A 100-year-old African-American woman tells her history by counting pennies in an old box. Each penny represents one year of her life. *See* HIGH INTEREST—LOW READING LEVEL.

Mayo, Margaret. **Mythical Birds & Beasts from Many Lands**. Illus. Jane Ray. Myths and legends using birds and animals from around the world are collected in this beautifully illustrated work. *See* MYTHS, FOLKTALES, AND LEGENDS.

McKissack, Patricia. **The Dark-Thirty: Southern Tales of the Supernatural**. Illus. Brian Pinkney. New York: Alfred A. Knopf, 1992. 122p. $15.00. ISBN 0-679-81863-4 (trade), 0-679-91863-9 (lib. bdg.).

Much can be learned about a culture or society by its stories and tales. McKissack has collected and recorded stories from her Southern African-American background that were originally passed down orally. This is a collection of 10 stories, each one based on some actual happening, but embellished and changed slightly with each retelling. Each story has a bit of mysticism or magic, and some are spooky and scary. All make great read alouds because they're written as though the storyteller is telling them and each includes an historical explanation of why and how the story evolved. The large scratchpad illustrations are expressive and add to the effectiveness of the book. This valuable collection of stories should be shared and enjoyed frequently with children.

Mikaelsen, Ben. **Sparrow Hawk Red**. A young boy crosses into Mexico and poses as a homeless child in an effort to infiltrate a drug cartel and avenge his mother's death. The story includes excellent descriptions of life on the streets in Mexico. *See* READ ALOUDS.

Moeri, Louise. **The Forty-Third War**. Boston: Houghton Mifflin, 1989. 200p. $14.00. ISBN 0-395-50215-2.
> Wars have plagued regions of Central America for years and each conflict is complicated and brutal, inflicting tremendous amounts of suffering and pain on the common person. This story is told through the eyes of a young boy, Uno Ramirez, who is captured by soldiers to fight for their cause. The rigors and hardships of military life are vividly described as Uno is forced to learn everything there is about fighting and the responsibilities of being a soldier in just eight short days. On the ninth day his regiment's job is to destroy a village and everyone in it. Uno's young life changes dramatically because of this horrendous experience, but he is eventually sent home with the order that he must study and become a teacher, because education is more powerful than war. This unsettling, powerful book points out the futility of wars and conflicts and the power of peace.

Myers, Walter Dean. **Brown Angels: An Album of Pictures and Verse**. This beautiful collection of poetry and photographs celebrates African-American children. *See* POETRY.

Paulsen, Gary. **The Crossing**. New York: Dell, 1987. 114p. $10.00. ISBN 0-440-20582-4.
> The main aim in the life of Manny Bustos is to cross the border from Juárez, Mexico, to the United States, where he's convinced life will be better. Manny, a homeless child who will do anything for food and shelter, picks the pocket of Sergeant Robert Locke, a lonely Vietnam vet who finds solace in whiskey. Manny worms his way into the sergeant's heart, and after many meetings the sergeant offers to get a visa for him and take him across the border legally. However, four men of the streets attack the sergeant and Manny in an alley, and the sergeant uses the skills learned in combat to shoot and kill all four men but is himself mortally wounded. In a dying act, he gives his wallet to Manny with instructions to cross the border. This significant work points out the measures taken by desperate people to attempt to find a better life in the United States. It's a powerful novel with excellent descriptions of life for a street child in a Mexican border town.

———. **The Tortilla Factory**. Illus. Ruth Wright Paulsen. New York: Harcourt Brace & Company, 1995. 32p. $14.00. ISBN 0-15-292876-6.
> The simple text beautifully describes the process of the earth being prepared to plant corn, which is then harvested and ground into flour, made into tortillas, and eaten by the workers, giving them strength so

that they can work the earth and begin the cycle again. The text accompanies rich, expressive illustrations that beautifully depict the planting, growing, and eating process. The texture of the linen paper stands out, and the paint actually feels heavy and thick on the paper, giving the feel and look of original paintings. This story is also available in Spanish under the title *La Tortillerie*.

Perkins, Mitali. **The Sunita Experiment**. New York: Joy Street Books, 1993. 179p. $15.95. ISBN 0-316-69943-8.
Sunita Sen has the same problem as many students who come from another culture but are living in America. They are caught between two cultures, attempting to continue their original way of life but also trying to be a teenager in the United States. Sunita's family came from India but had found a balance of the two cultures that seemed to work. However, when her mother's parents arrived from India, everything fell apart because Sunita's mother felt they needed to do everything in the traditional way to please the grandparents, changing Sunita's life a great deal. Suddenly Sunita couldn't have boyfriends. She had to eat Indian food for every meal, and tension built up within the family until it became apparent that they had to compromise and go back to the balance they had acquired before the grandparents arrived. The author wrote the book from her own experiences growing up in India but eventually settling in the San Francisco Bay Area of California.

Preiss, Byron, ed. **The Best Children's Books in the World: A Treasury of Illustrated Stories**. New York: Harry N. Abrams, 1996. 319p. ISBN 0-8109-1246-5.
This rich collection of modern-day children's books from around the world gives insight into the stories and folklore that are important to a variety of countries. Each of the 15 stories is told in its original language and presented with the original art along with translations on the sides of the pages. The stories were collected from countries as varied as Belgium, Brazil, China, England, Germany, Russia, Ghana, Austria, Iran, Israel, New Zealand, Norway, Slovakia, Spain, Sri Lanka, and Switzerland. The introduction explains how the books were chosen and an introductory page at the beginning of each book familiarizes the reader with the author and illustrator and gives background information about the book. Further information with statistics about each book is found at the end of the book in addition to an Editors' Afterword. This is a useful book when studying other countries, and it gives excellent examples of artwork from around the world.

Sola, Michele. **Angela Weaves a Dream: The Story of a Young Maya Artist**. Photo. Jeffrey Jay Foxx. The importance and history of weaving in a Mayan village are described and photographed. *See* FINE ARTS.

Staub, Frank. **Children of the Yucatan**. Minneapolis, MN: Carolrhoda Books, 1996. 47p. (The World's Children). $15.00. ISBN 0-87614-984-0.

> The beauty of the Yucatan Peninsula of Mexico is vividly displayed with large, colorful photographs. The text includes a brief history of the area, the work, the play, and the culture of this ancient place with particular attention paid to the ruins of Uxmal and Chitzen Itza. A pronunciation guide and an index are included, making this an informative, eye-pleasing work.

Tan, Amy. **The Chinese Siamese Cat**. Illus. Gretchen Schields. New York: Macmillan, 1994. 32p. $16.95. ISBN 0-02-788835-5.

> Have you ever wondered how Siamese cats ended up with their color patterns of dark ears and tails? This delightful story tells about a grouchy and Foolish Magistrate who makes rules that make people unhappy and about a family of cats that resides in his lavish mansion who are required to write these rules using their pointed tails as writing brushes. Mama Miao and Baba Miao dip their tails into the lampblack and write out the magistrate's latest mean rule. One day the new rule says no one may sing until sundown. One of the kittens accidentally falls onto the desk and blots out the word *no* so the edict goes out that everyone must sing until sundown. This brings so much joy to the people and even rubs off onto the magistrate, who becomes a Wise Magistrate and repeals all his nasty rules. From then on the cats who had been perfectly white took on dark spots because of the ink the kitten fell into, giving them their coloring pattern.

Taylor, Mildred D. **Roll of Thunder, Hear My Cry**. This outstanding work is the story of a Black family living in Mississippi during the Great Depression. *See* SOCIAL STUDIES—UNITED STATES HISTORY.

Yep, Laurence. **Dragon's Gate**. This book accurately describes the part the Chinese immigrants played in the building of the transcontinental railroad. *See* SOCIAL STUDIES—UNITED STATES HISTORY.

Chapter 9
MYTHS, FOLKTALES, AND LEGENDS

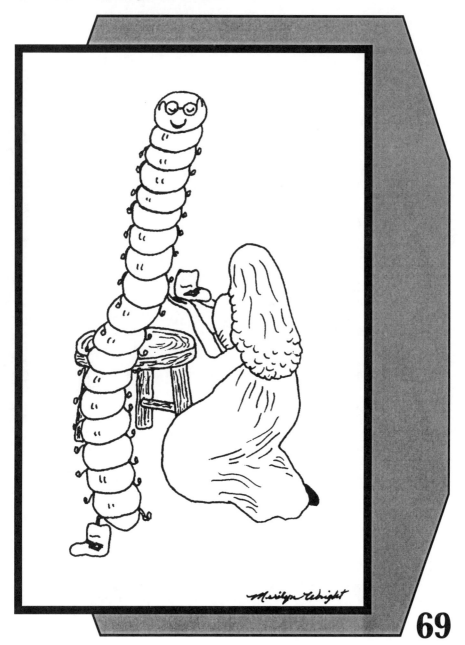

69

Throughout time people have enjoyed stories in the form of myths, folktales, and legends—usually based on something that happened to someone long ago but embellished and enhanced so that the truth becomes fantasy. A variety of stories are included in this section, many coming from other times and other countries but all a part of our literary culture.

Bahous, Sally. **Sitti and the Cats: A Tale of Friendship**. Niwat, Canada: Roberts Rinehart Publishers, 1993. 24p. $13.95. ISBN 1-879373-61-0.

Sitti, the kind, loving "grandmother" of the small Palestinian village, discovers a stranded kitten in a tree one cold, disagreeable winter day. She drops the bundle of sticks she had been gathering and rescues the kitten. The kitten takes Sitti to her home, where Sitti meets the entire cat clan. Here she is treated like royalty, fed well, and upon leaving is given a bag of garlic peels and a bag of onion peels. She puts these under her bed, and in the morning she discovers a bag of silver and a bag of gold rather than peelings. She immediately shares her wealth with anyone in the village who has needs. Her selfish friend, Im Yusuf, wants the same good fortune, goes to the cats, demands two bags of peelings, gets them, takes them home and puts them under her bed. To her amazement, the peelings turn into wasps and bees rather than coins, because good fortune comes only to those who make others happy. This book satisfies our quest to find good literature set in the Middle East. Along with the delightful story of Sitti, the author provides information about the mores, values, and customs of the area. Arabic terms are used and explained, and a glossary of terms is added at the end of the work. Boxes with explanations of terms, cities, and ideas are interspersed throughout with the text and the illustrations. The story is entertaining, but the added touches make this a valuable teaching tool.

Bateson-Hill, Margaret. **Lao Lao of Dragon Mountain**. Chinese text Manyee Wan, illus. Francesca Pelizzoli, paper cuts Sha-Liu Qu. This old Chinese folktale is told with Chinese paper cuts. *See* FINE ARTS.

Climo, Shirley. **Atalanta's Race: A Greek Myth**. New York: Clarion Books, 1995. 31p. $16.00. ISBN 0-395-67322-4.

Shunned at birth by her father because she isn't a boy, Atalanta is raised by a bear and later a hunter. Life on a mountaintop makes her an outstanding hunter and an especially talented runner. She finally leaves the mountain to compete in footraces throughout the land, and her true father, King Iasus, discovers who she is and brings her into his court. He insists she marry so that she can produce a son. In her quest for a husband, she challenges potential suitors to a footrace. If the suitor wins, he becomes her husband, but if he loses he loses his life. After many victories and still no husband, Aphrodite intercedes and helps Melanion to win. They are wed and love each other very much but forget to thank Aphrodite, so they are turned into a lion and a lioness by Rhea, Aphrodite's mother. This retelling of the famous Greek myth points out the power of the gods, the strength of love, and the importance of physical activity in the ancient Greek society. There are many Greek myths beautifully told, but Climo does an exceptional job of making this story exciting, accurate, and simple to read and understand; it will fit well with the study of the ancient Greeks. The Author's Notes describing the importance of physical competitions may be shared with physical-education classes.

————. **The Irish Cinderlad**. New York: HarperCollins, 1996. 32p. $14.95. ISBN 0-06-024396-1 (trade), 0-06-024397-X (lib. bdg.).

Many versions of "Cinderella" have been published recently, most using a female as the main character, but a male counterpart can also be found in "Cinderlad" stories from around the world. In this telling, Cinderlad, called Becan, is forced out of the house by his nasty stepmother and stepsisters and is rescued by a magical bull, rather than a fairy godmother. A variety of adventures and misadventures beset Becan until he rescues a princess. He accidentally leaves one of his boots behind, and the princess finds him a year later because he is the only one with feet large enough to fit into the boot.

Coburn, Jewell Reinhart, with Tzexa Cherta Lee. **Jouanah: A Hmong Cinderella**. Illus. Anne Sibley O'Brien. Arcadia, CA: Shen's Books, 1996. 32p. ISBN 1-885008-01-5 (English), 1-885008-02-3 (Spanish), 1-885008-03-1 (Hmong).

In this telling of the Hmong version of "Cinderella," the authors gathered together several versions of the story and created Jouanah, which means a young orphan, either male or female. A Hmong family in their native land need a cow, but there are none for sale. So the wife allows herself to become the family cow. Jouanah and her father sorely miss her mother, but with the help of the cow, the farm prospers. The father marries another woman with a daughter about Jouanah's age but when the stepmother discovers the real identity of the cow she becomes jealous and plans and schemes and causes the cow to die. Jouanah's father dies soon after, leaving her in the hands of the wicked stepmother, who makes her do all the household work and plays evil tricks on her, causing her life to be miserable. When it comes time for a big village celebration, Jouanah's mother becomes the fairy godmother, providing her with beautiful clothes, lovely jewelry, and a dainty pair of shoes. Jouanah attends the party, wins the heart of the most handsome man there, Shee-Nang, accidentally leaves one shoe behind when she has to hurry home, is eventually discovered by Shee-Nang, and they are married and live happily ever after. The illustrations depict Hmong culture, showing how they live, what they eat, and what they wear. A great deal of research went into this book to make it as authentic as possible and to show the richness of the culture. It is available in English, Spanish, and Hmong.

Delacre, Lulu. **Golden Tales: Myths, Legends, and Folktales from Latin America**. New York: Scholastic Press, 1996. 74p. $18.95. ISBN 0-590-48186-X.

This unusual collection of tales is from Latin America and includes old as well as new stories. The tales are from the Caribbean, the Taino Indians, Puerto Rico, the Dominican Republic, and Cuba; from Mexico; and from South America, including Colombia, Peru, Bolivia, and Chile. At the beginning of the book are an introduction and a map that explain why the stories were chosen. Each story is further introduced with an illustration and an introduction that explains the myth and the people it comes from. A paragraph included at the end of each story tells what happens next in the story or how this story still lives on today. The language flows beautifully, making these excellent read alouds.

Demi. **The Dragon's Tale and Other Animal Fables of the Chinese Zodiac**. New York: Henry Holt, 1996. 32p. $16.95. ISBN 0-8050-3446-3.

Each of the 12 animals in the Chinese zodiac is presented on a two-page spread with bright, beautiful, and descriptive illustrations. One page of the spread tells a tale about that animal, complete with a moral, and is surrounded by a circular illustration depicting the animal discussed. On the other page is another circular, brightly colored illustration intricately describing the activities presented in the tale. This work makes a perfect tie-in with the study of China, both ancient and present day.

————. **The Magic Tapestry**. New York: Henry Holt, 1994. 50p. $17.95. ISBN 0-8050-2810-2.

A poor Chinese widow weaves day and night for three years while her two oldest sons grumble, complaining about the time it is taking their mother to complete the tapestry and about their having to do menial work until it is ready to be sold. However, the third son understands his mother's need to make this perfect tapestry and happily works so that his mother is free to weave. When the tapestry is finally finished, the sons argue over who will sell it. A great wind blows it away, and the widow nearly dies from the shock. The sons go in different directions to find the weaving, and in true fairy tale style, the youngest son has the most difficult assignment but never gives up until he retrieves the tapestry and returns it to his mother. The weaving is so spectacular that the animals within it come to life, accompanied by the beautiful fairy princess the youngest son had met while on his search. Demi's vivid, colorful illustrations beautifully depict ancient Chinese drawings, customs, and traditions.

Hamilton, Virginia. **Her Stories: African American Folktales, Fairy Tales, and True Tales**. Illus. Leo Dillon and Diane Dillon. New York: The Blue Sky Press, 1995. 112p. $19.95. ISBN 0-590-47370-0 (trade), 0-590-56603-2 (lib. bldg.).

As is demonstrated by this collection of tales about African-American women celebrating the strength, dreams, and gift of life and love from generation to generation, Virginia Hamilton is unequaled when it comes to telling tales. The stories are divided into five sections: animal tales, fairy tales, the supernatural, folkways and legends, and true tales. Each story is a narrative about women in traditional Black folklore from around the world and is retold using rich, imaginative language. The stories make wonderful read alouds because of the colorful language.

Hastings, Selina. **Sir Gawain and the Loathly Lady**. New York: Mulberry Books, 1985. 29p. $4.95. ISBN 0-688-07046-9pa.

There are many renditions of King Arthur and his court. Arthur and his men are involved in extensive adventures in some. Others seem to adhere closely to the original tales. While still others seem quite far-fetched. This version has become a classic retelling, combining adventure, the Black Knight, a lovely princess, and Guinevere while giving insight about life in King Arthur's court. King Arthur is separated from his men while hunting and is accosted by the Black Knight, who says he will spare Arthur's life if he can answer a riddle: What is it that women most desire? The only woman who is able to give him the correct answer is a loathly old hag, gnarled and grotesque in every way. The payment for the answer is the promise that one of the men from Author's court will marry her. Sir Gawain, a truly gallant knight, agrees to marry the Loathly Lady, who, after the wedding, turns out to be a beautiful princess. The illustrations are plentiful and descriptive, making the book a beautiful source when studying the Middle Ages.

Kimmel, Eric A. **The Three Princes: A Tale from the Middle East**. Illus. Leonard Everett Fisher. New York: Holiday House, 1994. 32p. $16.00. ISBN 0-8234-1115-X.

A beautiful princess can't decide which of her three suitors to marry, so she sends them out to search for the rarest wonder they can find. Through this often-used but fascinating premise the reader experiences the life and the landscape of the Middle East. Leonard Everett Fisher does a remarkable job depicting this part of the world, which makes the book a valuable addition to the study of early cultures of the Middle East.

Kurtz, Jane. **Miro in the Kingdom of the Sun**. Illus. David Frampton. New York: Houghton Mifflin, 1996. 32p. $15.95. ISBN 0-395-69181-8.

An Inca prince is ill and can only be healed with water from Pachap Cuchun Cuchun, a mysterious lake that is hidden and difficult to find.

The soldiers and young men search day and night but cannot find the lake. Miro, a swift and strong young woman, wants to be able to do what her brothers do, but girls are only allowed to weave and do women's work. Headstrong and determined, she decides to search for the lake and is aided by the birds, who give her their best feathers so that she can fly to the lake. At the lake she is beset by many dangerous foes, but she uses the magic from the feathers to overcome the dangers and succeeds in her quest for water for the prince. After drinking it he becomes well, and Miro, though offered a life of luxury at the palace decides to return to her humble home after all her travels. The story is lovely, but it is an especially important telling because the author adds many aspects of Inca empire life. Through this story and with the help of the bold, colorful woodcuts, the reader learns about the animals, foods, clothing, customs, and surroundings of the Inca empire before the Spaniards' arrival. Many Indian words are used and are italicized for easy recognition.

Louie, Ai-Ling. **Yeh-Shen: A Cinderella Story from China**. Illus. Ed Young. New York: Philomel Books, 1982. 31p. $15.95. ISBN 0-399-20900-X.

This ancient Chinese version of "Cinderella" has been around since the days of the Tang dynasty. The author's family has passed this story down through the generations, but the story is also recorded in an ancient Chinese manuscript, included in the front of the book. Yeh-Shen is raised by a wicked stepmother and not allowed to go to the spring festival. An old man, a fairy godfather, appears and instructs her to ask favors of the remains of her pet fish that the stepmother had killed. These favors are granted, and Yeh-Shen is the hit of the festival. True to the tale, she flees hurriedly, leaves a tiny shoe behind, and is finally discovered by the king, marries, and lives happily ever after. The tale is surprisingly similar to the European "Cinderella." Chinese customs, dress, and landscape are vividly depicted with Ed Young's illustrations. The introduction, which gives an explanation of the work, is especially valuable when studying ancient China.

Mayo, Margaret. **Mythical Birds and Beasts from Many Lands**. Illus. Jane Ray. New York: Dutton Children's Books, 1997. 108p. $19.99. ISBN 0-525-45788-7.

This beautiful book combines myths and legends from many cultures and countries with the animals from those lands that are symbolically significant in that society. The reader encounters the Pegasus from Greece; a mermaid from England; the unicorn, representing Europe as a whole; the thunderbird, the character in a Native American tale; a dragon from China; the sea serpent from Scandinavia; a feathered snake from Latin America; the Minotaur from Greece; a snake, tiger, crow, and alligator from Burma; and the phoenix from Egypt. The language in the stories flows well, making them excellent read alouds. Small, brightly colored illustrations are scattered throughout the text along with some full-page illustrations. Stories from this book may be used at every grade level when studying other cultures and countries of the world or as examples of literature from around the world.

Patent, Dorothy Hinshaw. **Quetzal, Sacred Bird of the Cloud Forest**. The Quetzal bird, important in Central American folklore and culture, is presented in fact and fiction. *See* SOCIAL STUDIES—ANCIENT AND EARLY CULTURES.

San Souci, Robert D. **The Red Heels**. Illus. Gary Kelley. New York: Dial Books, 1996. 32p. $16.00; ISBN 0-8037-1133-6 (trade), 0-8037-1134-4 (lib. bdg.).

Jonathan Dowse, a traveling cobbler in colonial New England, falls in love with one of his customers, Rebecca. She possesses magical shoes with red heels that allow her to dance in the sky by moonlight. After discovering this rare attribute, Jonathan learns to dance with her. They marry, settle down, and have a family but continue to dance when the stars are out and the moon is high. This delightful tale shows what life was like during this time period, describing food, clothing, and housing, but it adds a new twist filled with fun and love. Speculation of witchcraft can be considered with a new perspective. The full-page illustrations are mystical and add to the mystery and magic of the story. This delightful yet thought-provoking tale ties in beautifully with the study of colonial America.

————. **Sootface: An Ojibwa Cinderella Story**. Illus. Daniel San Souci. New York: Doubleday Books for Young Readers, 1994. 32p. $15.95. ISBN 0-385-31202-4.

Sootface, the youngest of three motherless girls, is made to do all the hard work, bringing in water, tending the fire, and cooking and cleaning, while her two older sisters bark orders and make fun of her. Their father is gone during the day, so he isn't aware of the mistreatment, but throughout all her difficulties, Sootface keeps a positive attitude and is sure that someday she will find a husband. A brave but invisible hunter and warrior lives nearby, along with his sister. They begin a quest to find a wife for him, and the women from the village are invited to be interviewed, but they must identify what material is strung on his bow. None of the village women are able to see the warrior and his bow, so they answer incorrectly and are disqualified. Finally Sootface visits the hunter and is able to see his bow and identify that it is made from a rainbow and white fire, winning the warrior's hand in marriage. This is a delightful story, giving a good picture of what life was like in the Native American villages. The San Souci brothers' well-researched story and illustrations make the story historically accurate and authentic.

Shepard, Aaron. **Savitri: A Tale of Ancient India**. Morton Grove, IL: Albert Whitman & Company, 1992. Unpaged. $17.00. ISBN 0-8075-7251-9.

> This ancient Indian tale, a retelling of a part of India's most famous epic, *The Mahabharata*, centers around love, devotion, inner beauty and virtue, and marriage. An Indian king from long ago has many wives but no children. After praying for 18 years, he is finally granted a daughter, Savitri. She is beautiful inside and out, and when it is time for her to marry, her father allows her to go out into the land and choose her own husband. She travels far and wide and finally finds the perfect man, Prince Satyavan, in a hermitage, a place of prayer and study. In marrying him she is obliged to move to the hermitage and give up her luxurious life in the palace, which she is willing to do. A holy seer predicts that Satyavan has only one year to live, but because of her great love for the prince, Savitri chooses to spend that year with him. When Yama, the god of death, arrives to take Satyavan, Savitri bargains with him. Yama is willing to grant her wishes, but he refuses to give Satyavan's life back. Her final wish is to have many children with Satyavan and Yama grants this wish—meaning he must also give Satyavan back if he is to father children. This beautiful story of love and devotion is highlighted with colorful, vibrant illustrations that depict life in ancient India.

Stanley, Diane. **Fortune**. New York: Morrow Junior Books, 1990. 32p. $12.95. ISBN 0-688-07210-0 (trade), 0-688-07211-9 (lib. bdg.).

> Omar, a poor farmer's son, buys a dancing tiger that he names Fortune, because as he travels from city to city attracting crowds, he collects large sums of money, thus becoming a wealthy man. Omar soon forgets his old friends, especially Sunny, the love of his life who is waiting to marry him. His travels take him to a faraway city, where the weeping princess lives. She weeps because she lost her prince the day before their wedding. Unbeknownst to anyone, the evil witch, Jahnah, had turned the prince into a dancing tiger. When Omar presents Fortune to the princess, she hugs him, and the tiger is transformed back into the beautiful prince. Omar is rewarded with a fortune from the king. He returns to Sunny, marries her, and they live happily as the princess and prince. The story is simple, predictable, and enjoyable, and the illustrations are exquisite. They beautifully depict ancient Persian life, including clothing, buildings, food, and landscape.

Tompert, Ann. **Grandfather Tang's Story: A Tale Told with Tangrams**. This is an ancient Chinese folktale told using tangrams. *See* MATHEMATICS.

Williams, Laura E. **The Long Silk Strand: A Grandmother's Legacy to Her Granddaughter**. Illus. Grayce Bochak. In this story from ancient Japan, Grandmother saves pieces of silk thread, which she ties together into a large ball. After her death, the granddaughter grabs the end of the long thread to go to Grandmother and learns to say her final farewells. *See* SOCIAL STUDIES—ANCIENT AND EARLY CULTURES.

Williams, Marcia. **The Iliad and the Odyssey**. This cartoon presentation of the age-old stories makes them easy to understand as well as entertaining. *See* UNIQUE PRESENTATIONS.

Wisniewski, David. **Rain Player**. This original Mayan story involves the rain god, Chac, the jaguar, the quetzal, the *cenote*, and the game *pok-a-tok*. *See* SOCIAL STUDIES—ANCIENT AND EARLY CULTURES.

———. **The Warrior and the Wise Man**. The age-old struggle between strength and wisdom is presented in this twelfth-century Japanese story. *See* SOCIAL STUDIES—ANCIENT AND EARLY CULTURES.

———. **The Wave of the Sea-Wolf**. This original Tlingit myth set in the Pacific Northwest is based on a collection of stories gleaned from that culture. *See* SOCIAL STUDIES—UNITED STATES HISTORY.

Yep, Laurence. **The City of Dragons**. Illus. Jean Tseng and Mou-sien Tseng. New York: Scholastic, 1995. 32p. $14.95. ISBN 0-590-47865-6.

> A young village boy has a sad face because of a physical defect. No one in the village wants him around because he depresses them, so he runs away. He is befriended by a group of giants leading a caravan of large elephants. They take him with them on their surreal adventures. They travel under the ocean and meet giant clams, crabs, and sharks and come to a town of underwater dragons. All these strange creatures accept the boy, even though he has a sad and unusual face. In fact, the dragons want to be made sad because they make their living from pearls shed as tears by dragon maidens, and the dragons have run out of sad stories to make the maidens cry. The dragon maidens become sad looking at the boy, and they fill many bowls with pearl tears. The giants and the dragons are so thankful that they take the boy home, sending many bolts of silk and a sack of pearls with him. He is then accepted by his village, and they promise never to get upset about his looks again. This unusual tale teaches valuable lessons about life and depicts Chinese village life and the countryside.

———. **The Khan's Daughter: A Mongolian Folktale**. Illus. Jean Tseng and Mou-sien Tseng. New York: Scholastic Press, 1997. 32p. $16.95. ISBN 0-590-48389-7.

> A poor man's son sets out to marry the king's daughter and is assigned three difficult tasks to win her. In the end he overcomes each obstacle set before him. This is an age-old theme, but this time the setting is

Mongolia, the poor man's son is a sheepherder, and the king is the Khan. The language beautifully describes life specific to early Mongolia, with passages such as "domed tents spread all the way to the horizon like so many buttons sewn onto a giant sheet of brown felt." The illustrations are detailed and are unmistakably Mongolian. The landscape, the people and their homes, clothing, food, transportation, and activities are intricately drawn. The decorations on the clothing—particularly the daughter's headdress—are outstanding. It is unusual to have literature about Mongolia, so this is a real treasure.

Zeman, Ludmila. **Gilgamesh the King**. Plattsburgh, NY: Tundra Books of Northern New York, 1992. 24p. $20.00. ISBN 0-88776-283-2.

The story of Gilgamesh is one of the oldest stories in the world, first recorded onto clay tablets 5,000 years ago. French and British archaeologists first found some of the clay tablets in the nineteenth century and translated the cuneiform writing. This retelling, the first in a series of three books, finds the king of Uruk, Gilgamesh, half god and half man, unhappy and lonely. To prove his power he orders a massive wall to be built around the city. He forces the people to work long hours day after day, pushing them to exhaustion and despair until they finally ask for help from the sun god. As a result, another strong man, Enkidu, is sent to Earth but lives only with the animals and doesn't know about humans until Shamhat, the singer, is sent by Gilgamesh to lure him to Uruk so Gilgamesh can kill him. Shamhat teaches Enkidu about love, and they go back to Uruk, and Enkidu and Gilgamesh battle. Enkidu wins, but because he knows about love, he saves Gilgamesh, the two become fast friends, and Gilgamesh finally understands what it means to be a human. Work on the wall is stopped, and a new peace settles over Uruk. The full-page color illustrations are outstanding and depict Mesopotamian life in fine detail. The author and illustrator, Ludmila Zeman, did extensive research of artifacts at museums scattered throughout the world to re-create this epic tale.

————. **The Last Quest of Gilgamesh**. Plattsburgh, NY: Tundra Books of Northern New York, 1995. 32p. $20.00. ISBN 0-88776-328-6.

The epic tale of Gilgamesh dates back more than 5,000 years and is set in Mesopotamia. In this volume—the third and final book in the series—Gilgamesh attempts to overcome death. This quest takes him over the Mashu Mountain as he attempts to reach the sun god. Along the way he encounters an array of monstrous scorpions and other terrifying creatures. The sun god refers him to Utnapishtim, which requires a trip across the impossible Waters of Death, which swallow anything that touches them. He finally reaches Utnapishtim, but he must pass the test of staying awake for six days and six nights. He falls asleep, therefore failing the test, but he is given a plant that will keep him young as long as he is alive. He encounters the evil serpent, Ishtar, along the way and is tricked out of the magic plant. He ends up with his dear friend, Enkidu, and they fly back to Uruk. Enkidu points out to Gilgamesh that there is nothing that will allow him to live forever, but his immortality will be seen in the magnificent city he has built. The illustrations in all three books in the series are magnificent and fill every page with action, color, and detail.

———. **The Revenge of Ishtar**. Plattsburgh, NY: Tundra Books of Northern New York, 1993. 32p. $16.00. ISBN 0-88776-315-4.

In the second book in the Gilgamesh epic, the peace and happiness in Uruk is disturbed by an attack by the monster, Humbaba, which historians believe was a volcano in the surrounding mountains. The attack causes buildings to collapse, and the precious singer, Shamhat, is killed. Gilgamesh and Enkidu search out and destroy the monster, attracting the attention of the goddess Ishtar. When Gilgamesh rejects her, she attacks and intends to destroy Uruk, riding the Bull of Heaven, but Gilgamesh and Enkidu destroy the bull and incur even more anger from Ishtar. She sends another monster, an illness, which kills Enkidu, causing Gilgamesh to see death as the last monster to be destroyed, which is the topic of the third and final book. The artwork in this series is authentic and outstanding as seen in the opening pages of the book which show a game being played with large, decorated pieces. All the pieces of this game have actually been recovered and can be seen in the British Museum in London. Ludmila Zeman, the author and illustrator, uses the decorations from this game throughout the book, on the endpapers, and around the borders. This series is a must when studying the early civilizations of the Mesopotamian area.

Chapter 10

POETRY

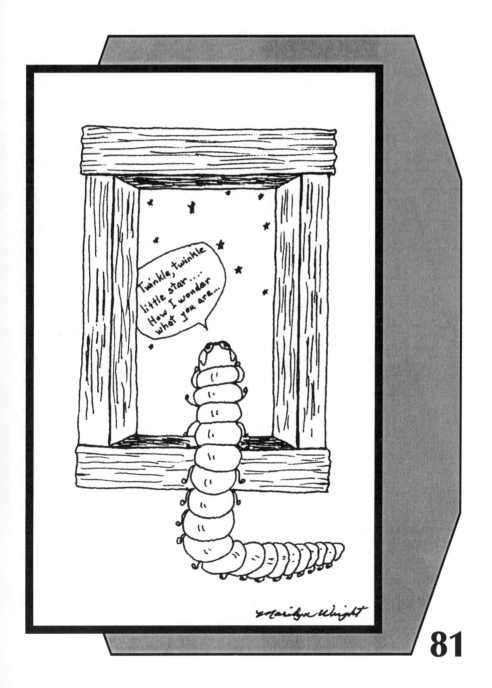

Poetry has the ability to express thoughts and feelings in a way that touches and delights all ages. The entries listed often tie in with curricula, but many of them should be enjoyed for the sheer pleasure of poetry and language.

Ada, Alma Flor. **Gathering the Sun: An Alphabet in Spanish and English**. Trans. Rosa Zubizarreta, illus. Simón Silva. This collection of poetry with one poem for each letter of the alphabet, is about Mexican-American farmworkers and is written in Spanish and English. *See* MULTICULTURAL.

Adoff, Arnold. **Love Letters**. Illus. Lisa Desimini. New York: The Blue Sky Press, 1997. Unpaged. $15.95. ISBN 0-590-48478-8.

The innocence and silliness of children is captured in this delightful collection of love poems written to various family members, classmates, the teacher, the family pets, and even to the writer of the poems. Each poem is meaningful yet light and humorous as seen in the one to Mom, which encourages her to "keep momming." The entry to the big brother acknowledges that he'll always be the oldest, but the writer likes it best when he listens and doesn't hit. The poems to classmates express the way students feel about one another. The brightly colored, whimsical illustrations fill the entire book, giving it a rich, full feeling.

Angelou, Maya. **Life Doesn't Frighten Me**. Illus. Jean-Michel Basquiat. New York: Stewart, Tabori & Chang, 1993. Unpaged. $16.00. ISBN 1-55670-288-4.

Maya Angelou's poetry reading at the inaugural swearing-in ceremony of President Clinton in 1993 brought her life and her work to the forefront, and many students are becoming more aware of her importance. This poem is an outstanding example of her philosophy of life. No matter what besets you—a barking dog, ghosts, dragons, tough guys, strangers, a new classroom, frogs, or snakes—use your own magic charm, learn to overcome obstacles, and life won't frighten you. The message is simple but powerful, made even more powerful with Jean-Michel Basquiat's artwork. Each page is filled with his avant-garde, brilliantly colored, splashy work. Biographies of Maya Angelou and Jean-Michel Basquiat are included at the end of the book along with a selected bibliography of Angelou's books and museums where Basquiat's works can be viewed.

Berry, James, ed. **Classic Poems to Read Aloud**. New York: Kingfisher, 1995. 256p. $16.95. ISBN 1-85697-987-3.

    This outstanding anthology of poems from all over the world, from all time periods, and with an unusual mix of poets lends itself to being read aloud. James Berry, the collector, went to great lengths to make this an extraordinary collection. Its broad categories offer a wide range of works, including quotes from the Bible and Shakespeare as well as poems by Shel Silverstein and Jack Prelutsky. This valuable addition to any classroom is the perfect book to pick up and read to a class when you have a few extras minutes at the end of a class or whenever you want to share good poetry.

Carlson, Lori M., ed. **Cool Salsa: Bilingual Poems on Growing Up Latino in the United States**. Intro. Oscar Hijuelos. Each of the entries in this collection of poetry is written by a Latino living in the United States but still practicing his or her Latino heritage. Each is written in Spanish and English. *See* MULTICULTURAL.

Carroll, Lewis. **Jabberwocky**. The famous poem from *Alice's Adventures in Wonderland* uses nonsense words in all the right places to tell a story. *See* ENGLISH—USE OF LANGUAGE.

Cumpián, Carlos. **Latino Rainbow: Poems About Latino Americans**. Biographies about Latino Americans are written in poem form. *See* MULTICULTURAL.

Demi. **Demi's Secret Garden**. New York: Henry Holt, 1993. Unpaged. $19.95. ISBN 0-8050-2553-7.

    Demi's collection of short, classic poems by a wide range of poets from a variety of countries includes 19 different insects frequently found in gardens and yards and illustrates each with large, colorful paintings that feature patterned papers embellished with gold. The print is large, and most poems fill a two-page spread. Several have pages that fold, so the insect spreads over three paint-filled pages. The Bird Wing Butterfly is so large it requires two fold-out pages, spreading the design over four pages. The poetry selections are excellent, and the artwork makes this book a feast for the eyes. In the Afterword, Demi gives a paragraph of explanation about each insect.

Ho, Minfong. **Maples in the Mist: Children's Poems from the Tang Dynasty**. Illus. Jean Tseng and Mou-sien Tseng. New York: Lothrop, Lee & Shepard, 1996. 32p. $15.00. ISBN 0-688-14723-2.

    Minfong Ho grew up learning Tang poems in Chinese, and she was fearful that her children's generation would lose them because they didn't want to struggle to learn the Chinese language and characters. She decided to translate them into English but includes the Chinese characters around the edges of the pages and in the illustrations. Each poem was originally written by a famous Tang poet and a short biography of each of these poets is included at the end of the book. Chinese traditions and life are represented on each two-page spread, beautifully illustrated with watercolors. This book is an outstanding tool to use when studying ancient China.

Hopkins, Lee Bennett. **Marvelous Math: A Book of Poems**. Math is seen in a unique manner with each of the 16 poems about mathematics. *See* MATHEMATICS.

————. **Opening Days: Sports Poems**. Illus. Scott Medlock. Poems about a variety of popular sports make up this poetry collection. *See* SPORTS AND GAMES.

Hopkins, Lee Bennett, selected by. **Extra Innings: Baseball Poems**. This is a collection of 19 poems about baseball. *See* SPORTS AND GAMES.

Huck, Charlotte. **Secret Places**. Illus. Lindsay Barrett George. New York: Greenwillow, 1993. 32p. $15.00. ISBN 0-688-11669-8 (trade) 0-688-11670-1 (lib. bdg.).

   Each poem in this collection explores a special place—real or imagined—that is dear to the poet's heart. This is a lovely collection of poetry by outstanding poets, including Elizabeth Coatsworth, Nancy Dingman Watson, bp Nichol, Myra Cohn Livingston, A. A. Milne, Dorothy Aldis, Aileen Fisher, Rachel Field, David McCord, Lois Simmie, Marchette Chute, Rose Burgunder, Byrd Baylor, Gwendolyn Brooks, and Karla Kuskin. Each poem paints a vivid image of the place being described, and the places vary widely: a favorite maple tree, a special locked box where treasures such as baseball cards and toys are kept, a hideout among some trees, a chair house made by throwing a blanket over an upended chair, a special rock, a sandy gully cutting through the Texas earth, or a good book. The brightly colored, vivid illustrations depict children younger than middle schoolers, but this doesn't detract from the usefulness and beauty of the collection.

Hudson, Wade. **Pass It On: African-American Poetry for Children**. Illus. Floyd Cooper. New York: Scholastic, 32p. $14.95. ISBN 0-590-45770-5.

   Each of the 19 poems in this collection, written by 14 outstanding African-American poets captures an aspect of the African-American experience. The oral tradition has always been strong in this culture, and poetry helps to keep that tradition alive. Some of the entries are just plain fun, as in "Prickled Pickles Don't Smile"; some are inspirational, such as "I Can"; and some, including "Harriet Tubman," are informative.

Wade Hudson was careful to include sad, silly, and serious poems as well as poems of self-affirmation and self-discovery. The paragraphs at the end of the book about each poet, the compiler, and the artist are helpful.

Myers, Walter Dean. **Brown Angels: An Album of Pictures and Verse**. New York: HarperCollins, 1993. 40p. $15.89. ISBN 0-06-022917-9 (trade), 0-06-022918-7 (lib. bdg.).

The beauty of African-American children is celebrated in the 12 poems collected in this work. The poems are upbeat and were inspired by Walter Dean Myers's collection of black-and-white photographs of African-American children around the turn of the century. Each one captures children at their best—with big smiles on their faces, dressed in their finest, ready for the photographer. The book gives the reader the feeling of looking through a family's photo album, making it personal and joyful. Several photographs accompany each poem, making this a visual as well as a literary treat.

Panzer, Nora, ed. **Celebrate America in Poetry and Art**. Famous artwork along with outstanding American poetry help to tell America's story. *See* FINE ARTS.

Parker, Nancy Winslow. **Locks, Crocs, & Skeeters: The Story of the Panama Canal**. The story of the Panama Canal is told through poetry. *See* UNIQUE PRESENTATIONS.

Prelutsky, Jack. **The Dragons Are Singing Tonight**. Illus. Peter Sis. New York: Greenwillow, 1993. 39p. $15.00. ISBN 0-688-09645-X (trade), 0-688-12511-5 (lib. bdg.).

Combine one the funniest poets of our time, Jack Prelutsky, with a favorite topic of many students, dragons, add a top illustrator, Peter Sis, and you end up with a superb book. Each poem has a dragon as the main character, but each dragon has its own personality and characteristics. In "I'm an Amiable Dragon" the dragon is a nice guy and doesn't want anyone to dislike him. In "I Made a Mechanical Dragon" the dragon is made from scraps and doesn't always work exactly right. "Nasty Little Dragonsong" features a half-inch-high dragon that is nasty to everyone at all times. In "A Dragon's Lament" the dragon is tired of being a dragon and wants to stop being "despicable, ruthless and fierce" and to rid himself of his bad reputation. Each poem is set on a full-page color illustration, which adds to the humor or horror. These are especially good when read aloud.

————. **The Random House Book of Poetry for Children**. Illus. Arnold Lobel. New York: Random House, 1983. 248p. $15.95. ISBN 0-394-85010-6 (trade), 0-394-95010-0 (lib. bdg.).

This exceptional collection of children's poetry has been out for a few years, but nothing has been published since that surpasses it. It includes 572 poems organized into 14 topics. Jack Prelutsky's choices vary from hilarious to serious, from those that simply tell to highly descriptive poems, and from those that have stood the test of time to some newly minted gems. Favorites such as Diane Siebert's rhythmic "Train Song," Carl Sandburg's "Arithmetic," and "A Visit from St. Nicholas" by Clement Moore are included as well as hundreds of other equally useful and appropriate poems. Every teacher and parent at all grade levels ought to own this book and pull it off the shelf with regularity.

Rosen, Michael. **Walking the Bridge of Your Nose**. Illus. Chloë Cheese. A collection of rhymes, riddles, tongue twisters, puns, word games, wordplay, limericks, and word puzzles that will delight all who encounter the book. *See* ENGLISH—USE OF LANGUAGE.

Sandburg, Carl. **Arithmetic: Illustrated As an Anamorphic Adventure by Ted Rand**. Illus. Ted Rand. The poem "Arithmetic" is illustrated with anamorphic images. *See* MATHEMATICS.

Schertle, Al. **Advice for a Frog**. Illus. Norman Green. Fourteen animals from around the world are presented in poetry form along with powerful illustrations. *See* SCIENCE.

————. **Keepers**. Illus. Ted Rand. New York: Lothrop, Lee & Shepard, 1996. 32p. $16.00. ISBN 0-688-11654-3.
From the ordinary topics such as "My Old Dog" and "May Is" to the unusual—"A Silver Trapeze" and "Keeper"—the author uses beautiful language to present simple ideas. Each poem is short, yet portrays the subject lyrically. Ted Rand's illustrations are colorful and descriptive and fit the poetry perfectly. There is something for everyone in this beautiful collection.

Schwartz, Alvin. **And the Green Grass Grew All Around: Folk Poetry from Everyone**. Rhymes, wordplay, songs, riddles, and chants make up this collection of 250 folk poems. *See* READ ALOUDS.

Siebert, Diane. **Sierra**. Illus. Wendell Minor. The Sierra Nevada of California are celebrated with beautiful poetry and breathtaking illustrations. *See* SCIENCE.

Silverstein, Shel. **Falling Up**. New York: HarperCollins, 1996. 171p. $16.00. ISBN 0-06-024802-5, 0-06-024803-3 (lib. bdg.).
Children everywhere love Shel Silverstein and his two most famous works, 1974's *Where the Sidewalk Ends* and 1981's *A Light in the Attic*.

This book of poetry, written in the same vein as the two previous favorites, includes drawings and poetry that seem familiar because the same format is used. The poetry is just as funny and silly, making this another winner. Silverstein is a master at taking a somewhat normal incident or object and making it crazy and bizarre. In "Snowball" the narrator likes the snowball he made so much that he takes it to bed with him. However, it runs away after wetting the bed. The title poem, "Falling Up," presents a child who trips on his shoelace and falls up rather than down. It makes him sick to his stomach, so he throws down. Readers will soon find themselves chuckling while reading this latest collection.

Spivak, Dawnine. **Grass Sandals: The Travels of Basho**. Illus. Demi. New York: Atheneum Books for Young Readers, 1997. Unpaged. $16.00. ISBN 0-689-80776-7.
Basho was a seventeenth-century Japanese haiku poet who gave up the comforts of home and set out to walk throughout Japan, writing haiku as he went. He took with him only the bare necessities, which included grass sandals for walking. Along with the story of Basho's travels, his haiku is included on each two-page spread, as is the Japanese character that depicts the main idea of the poem. Demi shows the reader how such characters often look like the item they describe. For instance, the character for *mountain* resembles the shape of a mountain, or the Japanese word for *horse* has the action of a running horse. This is a perfect tie-in when studying early Japan.

Thayer, Ernest Lawrence. **Casey at the Bat: A Ballad of the Republic, Sung in the Year 1888**. Illus. Patricia Polacco. Illustrator Polacco adds a unique twist on the old, familiar, favorite poem. *See* SPORTS AND GAMES.

Turner, Ann. **Grass Songs**. Illus. Barry Moser. New York: Harcourt Brace Jovanovich, 1993. 51p. $16.95. ISBN 0-15-136788-4.
In the nineteenth century, when the man of the family decided to pull up stakes and move west, the wife and the children had little choice but to follow him. This collection of original poems was inspired by reading actual diaries and first-person accounts of women who moved west. Some were happy to be leaving, to be free of the restraints of civilization, as in the poem "Glad to Be Gone." The woman telling this story says she "never wept for home." In "No Time Enough," the wagon train can only stop for one day to wait for Rebecca Hartshorn to give birth to her baby. Unfortunately, Rebecca doesn't survive, but the baby does, causing even more problems for the train. In the entry "Olive Oatman" the reader learns that a woman is captured by Native Americans, marries a brave, has children, and loves her new life. Later she is found by White men and forced to go back to her other life, but she hates it and misses her Native American husband and three sons for the remainder of her life. This is a moving, powerful collection of poems that can accompany the study of the westward movement.

————. **Mississippi Mud: Three Prairie Journals**. Illus. Robert J. Blake. New York: HarperCollins, 1996. Unpaged. $15.95. ISBN 0-06-0244321 (trade), 0-06-024433-X (lib. bdg.).

The three oldest children—Amanda, Caleb, and Lonnie—all keep journals in the form of poetry as they travel from West Virginia to the Oregon Territory in the 1800s. Their thoughts, fears, hopes, and dreams are exquisitely told and cover a variety of topics from the time they leave to their arrival. After weeks of encountering no other people, they look forward to civilization, a town, but when they arrive it consists of only six people and two dogs. Even though they are on a grueling journey, Amanda and the other girls her age dream of love and other typical teenage concerns. Caleb has many fears, so he prepares for the journey by collecting and wearing a host of good-luck charms. Jake, the family dog, dies along the way because his body simply wears out, but the family mourns his passing the remainder of the journey. Caleb's fondest dream is to own a horse with a black mane, and he gets his wish by saving a horse from being whipped to death by its owner. Lonnie tells about the birth of a baby sister, Columbia. The family has to stop traveling and with no help from another woman or a doctor has to help Ma with the birth. The writing is straightforward but emotional and is exceptional because the events and stories are told from the children's point of view, not the adults. The artwork blends superbly with the text. The artist actually traveled the Oregon Trail in a Conestoga wagon to better understand the journey, the sights and scenery, and the ordeal. This book is an absolute must when discussing the westward movement.

Viorst, Judith. **If I Were in Charge of the World and Other Worries**. Illus. Lynne Cherry. New York: Atheneum, 1981. 56p. $15.00. ISBN 0-689-30863-9.

The 41 poems gathered together in this book have become classics because they say so much about children's lives and do so in a humorous manner—telling it just the way it is. This is a collection that has stood the test of time and should be included in every library and teacher's and parent's collection. The title poem, "If I Were in Charge of the World" is an excellent jumping-off piece that can be used in creative writing or simply enjoyed. All the poems in the collection will tickle the funny bone of children and adults because they all deal with subjects common to children. For instance, "Fifteen, Maybe Sixteen, Things to Worry About" is perfect for the worrywart in the crowd. "Short Love Poem" tells the plight of the shortest guy in the class who is in love with the tallest girl. Saying "I'm sorry" is always difficult, so everyone will be able to relate to "Apology," where trying to spit out the words "I'm sorry" or "I made a big mistake" or "please forgive me" causes the writer to faint. Children of all ages love this collection, but it seems especially appropriate for middle schoolers.

Chapter 11
READ ALOUDS

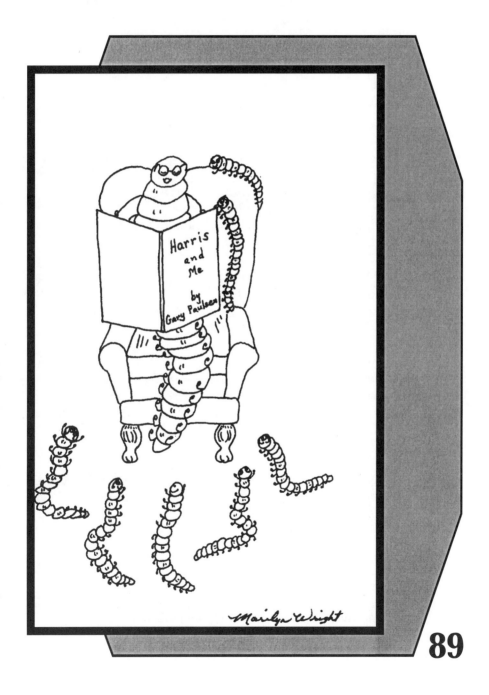

People of all ages love to be read to, but the material must be exciting and interesting enough to hold the listener's attention. The following is a list of books that have been found to give enjoyment to both the reader and the listener. Many of them may be connected with a specific curriculum, but others may be enjoyed simply for the joy of listening to a book.

———

Avi. **The True Confessions of Charlotte Doyle**. Charlotte, a 13-year-old, is the only female on a ship traveling from Liverpool, England, to Providence, Rhode Island, in 1832. The crew mutinies, and she is caught up in danger, mystery, and intrigue. The description of her climbing the rigging of the ship is so exciting and well told, it'll have listener's hands sweaty and hurting. *See* ENGLISH—CLASSICS.

———. **Wolf Rider: A Tale of Terror**. Andy receives a phone call from a man stating he just killed Nina. Andy feels compelled to solve the mystery and in doing so endangers himself. *See* HIGH INTEREST—LOW READING LEVEL.

Bauer, Marion Dane. **On My Honor**. Tony and Joel stop at a dangerous river for a swim even though they've been warned all their lives not to go in that river. Tony attempts to swim across the river, but doesn't make it. Joel has to live with Tony's death and has a difficult time telling the truth to his and Tony's parents. *See* HIGH INTEREST—LOW READING LEVEL.

Bennett, Jay. **Sing Me a Death Song**. New York: Franklin Watts, 1990. 131p. $15.00. ISBN 0-531-15115-8 (trade), 0-531-10853-8 (lib. bdg.), 0-449-70369-Xpa.

Jason Feldon's mother is on death row, with execution only days away. Everyone is convinced she committed the murder, including her own sister and her lawyer. However, Jason is sure she's innocent, especially after speaking with a dying policeman, who gives him some valuable information that indicates her innocence. He begins his own investigation, which takes him from New York City to Florida and involves him with dangerous criminals who have no regard for his life and will easily kill him if given the opportunity. Once this book is started, there's no stopping until Jason uncovers all the necessary facts.

Berry, James, selected by. **Classic Poems to Read Aloud**. This poetry anthology lends itself to being read aloud and begs to be picked up often and shared with children. *See* POETRY.

Bunting, Eve. **Someone Is Hiding on Alcatraz Island**. Danny Sullivan is being pursued by four Outlaw gang members out to kill him. They end up on Alcatraz Island overnight with no possible escape. It's a fast-paced, exciting story with new twists and turns on every page. *See* HIGH INTEREST—LOW READING LEVEL.

Byars, Betsy. **The Dark Stairs**. New York: Viking, 1994. 130p. (A Herculeah Jones Mystery). $13.90. ISBN 0-670-85487-5.

>This is the first in the Herculeah Jones Mystery Series, featuring Herculeah Jones, self-made detective. Her mother is a private investigator and her father a police detective, so she uses instinct, skills gained from her parents, and her own curiosity to solve dangerous and puzzling mysteries. Her sidekick and best friend, Meat, is pulled into the action against his will, which adds humor and even more danger because of his bumbling ways. Each chapter has a cliff-hanger ending which entices the listener to beg for more. Written on a fifth- and sixth-grade level, these are highly appealing to the younger middle-school students. In this episode Herculeah attempts to solve a murder that she suspects took place at an old, derelict estate, Dead Oaks. During the course of her snooping around, she and Meat are endangered and barely escape with their lives.

————. **Dead Letter**. New York: Viking, 1996. 147p. (A Herculeah Jones Mystery). $13.99. ISBN 0-670-86860-4.

>In a newly acquired secondhand coat, Herculeah Jones, a self-made detective, discovers a mysterious note that seems like a plea for help. She decides either a murder is about to take place or has already happened. In her usual fashion, she ignores the warnings given by her mother, a bona fide private investigator, and her father, a police detective, to disregard the note and stay out of trouble. She rallies help from her hilarious sidekick, Meat, and sets out to solve the mystery. This is the third book in the Herculeah Jones Series and is just as exciting and fun as the others. Each chapter has a cliff-hanger ending, which will keep students begging for more.

————. **Tarot Says Beware**. New York: Viking Press, 1995. 151p. (A Herculeah Jones Mystery). $13.99. ISBN 0-670-85575-8.

>Three clues alert Herculeah Jones that something is amiss at Madame Rosa's house. The door to her house is open, her parrot has flown outside unattended, and Herculeah's hair begins to frizzle. Based on these suspicions, she investigates and discovers Madame Rosa's body. Madame Rosa, a local fortune teller, was Herculeah's good friend, so Herculeah sets out to solve her murder, using her usual investigative instincts that

she inherited from her private-investigator mother and her police-detective father. She pulls her bumbling best friend, Meat, into the investigation and, using some rather unusual techniques, tracks down the killer, putting herself and Meat into dangerous situations. The story is humorous as well as scary, making it fun and frightening.

Carroll, Lewis. **Jabberwocky**. The famous poem from *Alice's Adventures in Wonderland* must be read aloud to determine its meaning. *See* ENGLISH—USE OF LANGUAGE.

Christopher, John. **The City of Gold and Lead**. New York: Macmillan, 1967. 218p. $13.00. ISBN 0-02-042701-8, 0-440-84282-4pa.

————. **The Pool of Fire**. New York: Macmillan, 1968. 178p. $13.00. ISBN 0-02-718350-5, 0-02-042721-2pa.

————. **The White Mountains**. New York: Macmillan, 1967. 184p. $14.00. ISBN 0-02-718360-2, 0-440-84292-1.
There are no wars in the world but neither is there travel nor communication outside of one's own village. After being "capped" by giant tripods in their thirteenth year, humans live, unquestioningly, in the style of the Middle Ages while the relics of the Ancients, the great cities and machines of the twentieth century, lie in silent ruins. A few months before his own capping ceremony, Will is recruited into joining a small band of uncapped who live far to the south in the White Mountains. He is joined by his cousin Henry and by a young Frenchman, Beanpole (Jean Paul). Their arduous and dangerous journey is a constant battle against capture, starvation, and disease. Will becomes seriously ill, and the three are subsequently taken prisoner in the Chateau de la Tour Rouge. Will has the good fortune to become a favorite of the Compte and Comptessa as well as their beautiful daughter, Eloise. At this point Will faces a serious temptation when he is offered the chance to become a nobleman and live the rest of his life in splendid luxury. He is shaken back to the reality and the importance of their mission when Eloise is taken—quite willingly—to serve the tripods, never to return. The three boys resume their journey, and after many harrowing adventures, including one in which they fight and destroy one of the gigantic tripods, eventually reach their destination, where they join the small band of men who plan to retake the Earth from the tripods. That story is told in the second and third book in the trilogy: *Pool of Fire* and *City of Gold and Lead*. The White Mountains trilogy is well written, with a sophisticated use of language, strong character development, and a wonderful plot with adventures that will keep the listener's and reader's attention. There is also a prequel to the trilogy, Christopher's 1988 work *When the Tripods Came*, which explains why the tripods were allowed to take over and conquer almost the entire Earth.

Curtis, Christopher. **The Watsons Go to Birmingham—1963**. A middle-class Black family from Detroit becomes involved in the civil-rights movement in Birmingham. *See* SOCIAL STUDIES—UNITED STATES HISTORY.

DeFelice, Cynthia. **Weasel**. New York: Macmillan, 1990. 119p. $12.95. ISBN 0-02-726457-2, 0-380-71358-6pa.

    Father goes off to hunt, leaving Nathan and Molly alone in the cabin in the wilds of Ohio in 1839. Father fails to return, and the children are frightened, cold, and hungry. Suddenly, in the dead of the night, there's a knock on the door. Nathan reluctantly opens it to find a large, shaggy, speechless man motioning them to follow him. They have no intention of going anywhere with this frightening stranger until he holds out their mother's locket—their father has worn this ever since their mother's death—meaning the man has some information about their father. So they agree to follow him. Along the way, the large man, Ezra, scratches the word Weasel in the dirt, which strikes terror in Nathan and Molly because they had heard their parents talk about the man who had been sent by the government to eradicate the Shawnee Indians. After killing every Shawnee possible, he turned on the settlers, killing for sport. As the story unfolds the children discover Ezra is living proof of Weasel's evilness, because Weasel killed Ezra's half-Native American wife and cut out Ezra's tongue, causing his speechlessness. Ezra takes the children to their father, who has been seriously injured by Weasel. Molly and Ezra nurse their father back to health while Nathan returns home to tend the animals. Weasel captures him, but Nathan escapes and after Father is well, they return home. Father does not want revenge, but Nathan is so obsessed with it that he disobeys his father and goes to Weasel's cabin, only to find he has died from injuries sustained while he was capturing Nathan. This fast-paced, easy-to-read thriller will keep readers on the edge of their seats. It gives an excellent picture of what life was like in the unsettled parts of the United States during the westward movement.

Delacre, Lulu. **Golden Tales: Myths, Legends, and Folktales from Latin America**. This outstanding collection of Latin American folktales includes explanations and maps. *See* MYTHS, FOLKTALES, AND LEGENDS.

Fitzgerald, John D. **The Great Brain Is Back**. Illus. Diane deGroat. After John Fitzgerald's death, an additional manuscript was found, working the ninth book in the Great Brain series about the antics of J. D. and his older brother, Tom, who uses his Great Brain to connive, swindle, and outwit the other kids in town. *See* GREATEST OF THE LATEST.

George, Jean Craighead. **My Side of the Mountain**. Sam gets tired of city life and goes to live in a hollow tree in the Catskill Mountains. He is able to survive by using scientific knowledge and common sense. *See* SCIENCE.

————. **On the Far Side of the Mountain**. The sequel to *My Side of the Mountain*. Sam's sister comes to live with him in his camp in the Catskill Mountains. *See* SCIENCE.

Hamilton, Virginia. **Her Stories: African American Folktales, Fairy Tales, and True Tales**. Illus. Leo Dillon and Diane Dillon. Every story in this collection is about Black women and their legacy to the culture. The rich colorful language is perfect for reading aloud. *See* MYTHS, FOLKTALES, AND LEGENDS.

Hobbs, Will. **Far North**. A small plane crashes and those who survive must endure the wilds of Canada during the winter. *See* SCIENCE.

Howard, Ellen. **The Log Cabin Quilt**. Illus. Ronald Himler. A family moves west to help them forget Mother's death, but it doesn't work until they survive a crisis and solve it by using quilt pieces to chink the logs in their little cabin. *See* SOCIAL STUDIES—UNITED STATES HISTORY.

Konigsburg, E. L. **The View from Saturday**. A unique group of children practice for and win the Academic Bowl. *See* GREATEST OF THE LATEST.

Lowry, Lois. **The Giver**. Jonas, a 12-year-old boy, becomes the Giver, the only person in a "perfect" society to remember a previous life. With knowledge, he begins to question the practices necessary to allow life to be perfect. *See* ENGLISH—CLASSICS.

Martinez, Victor. **Parrot in the Oven: Mi Vida/A Novel**. Mexican-American life in the California Central Valley is described in this collection of short stories. *See* MULTICULTURAL.

Mayo, Margaret. **Mythical Birds and Beasts from Many Lands**. Illus. Jane Ray. This collection contains 10 myths from around the world, each involving mythical animals. *See* MYTHS, FOLKTALES, AND LEGENDS.

McKissack, Patricia C. **The Dark-Thirty: Southern Tales of the Supernatural**. This is a collection of 10 African-American stories written the way they were told originally by storytellers. *See* MULTICULTURAL.

McMullan, Kate. **Under the Mummy's Spell**. A modern-day boy, Peter, meets a girl from ancient Egypt in the Metropolitan Museum of Art. She is a mummy, but Peter comes under her spell when he kisses her coffin. The chapters alternate between Peter's story, written in regular print and Nephia's story, which is printed in italics. *See* SOCIAL STUDIES—ANCIENT AND EARLY CULTURES.

Mikaelsen, Ben. **Sparrow Hawk Red**. New York: Hyperion Books for Children, 1993. 185p. $5.00. ISBN 0-7868-1105-6pa.

Flying is the one activity Ricky and his father, Benito, still enjoy doing together now that Ricky's mother is dead. Her death was so traumatic that Benito retired from his job as a Drug Enforcement Agent to care for Ricky. Her death becomes even more unbearable when strangers come to visit, and Ricky overhears that his mother was accidentally murdered by drug runners from Mexico. DEA officials want Benito to return to work to finish the job of finding this group in Mexico and to get back a radar-equipped plane stolen from the DEA. Benito refuses to go after the plane, which makes Ricky angry, so Ricky decides to do it himself. He secretly crosses the border and pretends to be a homeless child. In this way he thinks he can get inside information about the location of the drug cartel, sneak into their compound, and steal the plane, returning it to Texas. Life on the streets is a real eye-opener for Ricky, and he meets many interesting people. He's about to give up on his plan when he meets Soledad, an abused young girl who befriends him and helps him accomplish his mission. The story seems far-fetched, but when told through the eyes of an angry child willing to do anything to avenge the death of his mother, it makes sense. Ricky's adventures are dangerous, hair-raising, and suspenseful, making this a great read aloud. The descriptions of life on the streets in Mexico are excellent. Ben Mikaelsen won the California Young Reader's Medal for this book in 1997.

Naylor, Phyllis Reynolds. **Shiloh**. New York: Atheneum, 1991. 144p. $12.95. ISBN 0-689-31614-3.

A young, abused beagle wanders into Marty Preston's yard one day, and Marty instantly falls in love with it. His father, a mailman, knows the dog belongs to their unfriendly neighbor, Judd, so he insists they take the dog back to its owner, who immediately kicks the dog and ties it up. Marty makes a promise to himself that if the dog returns, he will not take him back to Judd. The dog, which he names Shiloh, does return, so Marty builds a secret fence for him in the back part of their property. However, one secret causes another, one lie causes another lie, and soon Marty is caught up in several dilemmas. There's no extra food for a dog at their house, so feeding Shiloh is a major problem. Keeping his little sister away and not letting his best friend, David, know about Shiloh is almost more than he can bear. The truth finally comes out, and Marty is forced to confront Judd about legally keeping the dog. This heartwarming story is sure to win the hearts of listeners. There is now a sequel, *Shiloh Season* (see Chapter 5, "Greatest of the Latest"), and a third and final book in the trilogy, *Saving Shiloh*, has recently been released.

North, Sterling. **Rascal: A Memoir of a Better Era**. The true story of the author and his pet raccoon, Rascal, is funny and delightful. *See* SCIENCE.

O'Brien, Robert C. **Mrs. Frisby and the Rats of NIMH**. This is a fantasy about a society formed by a group of rats that escaped from an intelligence-enhancing experiment at the National Institute of Mental Health. *See* ENGLISH—CLASSICS.

Paterson, Katherine. **Bridge to Terabithia**. This is a strong story of friendship and finding one's place in society that shouldn't be missed by middle schoolers. *See* ENGLISH—CLASSICS.

Paulsen, Gary. **Brian's Winter**. Brian is forced to survive in the wilds of Canada during the winter. This sequel to *Hatchet* assumes that Brian was not rescued in the summer. *See* SCIENCE.

———. **Harris and Me: A Summer Remembered**. New York: Harcourt Brace and Company, 1993. 157p. $13.95. ISBN 0-15-292877-4, 0-440-40994-2pa.
> In this somewhat autobiographical work Paulsen tells about the summer he spent with a devil-may-care cousin, Harris. In a hilarious fashion he relates one wild incident after another involving life on a farm in the 1930s. What one boy doesn't think of, the other does, and readers will find themselves laughing out loud when Paulsen tells of their misadventures when attempting to ride the bull or how he managed to finally get revenge on Harris by tricking him into urinating on the electric fence. Students will beg for more, never wanting you to stop reading.

———. **Hatchet**. A boy's plane crashes in the wilds of Canada, and his only tool to help him survive is a hatchet. *See* SCIENCE.

Prelutsky, Jack. **The Dragons Are Singing Tonight**. Illus. Peter Sis. Poetry about all types of dragons is the topic of this outstanding work. *See* POETRY.

———. **The Random House Book of Poetry for Children**. This is considered to be the best collection of poetry on the market at this time. *See* POETRY.

Rawls, Wilson. **Where the Red Fern Grows**. New York: Delacorte Press, 1961. 249p. $16.00. ISBN 0-553-27429-5.
> Billy, a 10-year-old boy in northeastern Oklahoma in the Ozarks, wants nothing more than a hunting pup. Times are tough, and he knows his parents can't afford to buy him one, so he does every odd job possible to earn money. He does so well he is able to purchase two redbone hound puppies, Old Dan and Little Ann. This is a delightful story about a boy who loves his dogs so much he's willing to make sacrifices in his own life to make sure his dogs are properly cared for and trained. This book makes a wonderful read aloud because it touches strong feelings that every child has had at one time or another. He is close to his parents and has a special bond with his grandfather who runs a general store in the nearest town. The book is humorous, touching, exciting, and sad and tends to stick with kids for a long time.

Reimer, Luetta, and Wilbert Reimer. **Mathematicians Are People, Too: Stories from the Lives of Great Mathematicians**. Short, easy-to-read biographies of 15 famous mathematicians are designed to be read aloud with the purpose of interesting students in mathematics. *See* MATHEMATICS.

Roberts, Willo Davis. **Twisted Summer**. New York: Atheneum Books for Young Readers, 1996. 156p. $15.00. ISBN 0-689-80459-8.
> If you're looking for an exciting mystery filled with intrigue plus a love story, try this one. Roberts always comes up with a good mystery, and this is no exception. Cici's family, like many other families around Crystal Lake, has spent the summers there year after year. This particular summer Cici, now almost 15, figures she'll be old enough to do the "big kids" activities, and she's hoping she'll have 17-year-old Jack's attention. However, a murder was committed on the island, and Jack's older brother, Brody, was accused of it, tried, and convicted. The incident has caused Jack to be distant and apart from the other kids, so Cici's hopes of Jack's attention dwindle. She sets out to search for the real murderer and comes up with some dangerous and surprising discoveries.

Rosen, Michael. **Walking the Bridge of Your Nose**. Illus. Chloë Cheese. This delightful collection of tongue twisters, riddles, puns, word games, wordplay, humorous rhymes, limericks, and word puzzles is begging to be read aloud to audiences of all ages. *See* ENGLISH—USE OF LANGUAGE.

Sachar, Louis. **There's a Boy in the Girl's Bathroom**. New York: Alfred A. Knopf, 1987. 195p. $11.95. ISBN 0-394-88570-8 (trade), 0-394-98570-2 (lib. bdg.), 0-394-80572-0pa.

> Every school seems to have a few students who don't seem to fit with everyone else, and no matter how hard they try, they gain attention because of their bizarre and outrageous behavior. Bradley Chalkers is the kid at Red Hill School who stands out and creates a stir. The school counselor, Carla, takes him under her wing and tries to change his behavior. Listeners will howl at Bradley's antics but also feel empathy for him because inside he feels so confused and unloved. Younger middle-school students love to have this read to them because they relate to the school setting and will see themselves somewhere in the book.

Schwartz, Alvin. **And the Green Grass Grew All Around: Folk Poetry from Everyone**. New York: HarperCollins, 1992. 193p. $15.00. 0-06-22757-5 (trade), 0-06-022758-3 (lib. bdg.).

> This marvelous collection of 300 poems, songs, chants, rhymes, and sayings is truly unique. Schwartz collected this "folk poetry" over the years from his own childhood, school playgrounds, and children from throughout the United States. He found certain "ditties" were chanted, told, and sung again and again, and he wanted them to be accessible in one collection. It's a slice of Americana seen through the eyes of children's sayings, some of them teasing and lovingly irreverent, others simply silly—but all of them fun. The reader is treated to some musical favorites, such as "Here comes the bride, big fat and wide," complete with music notations; "On Top of Old Smoky," "On top of Spaghetti," and "The Ants Go Marching One by One"; and some rhythmic jump-roping chants and ball-bouncing rhymes and riddles and limericks. This collection is a well-researched, well-documented work with 43 pages of notes and sources and a thorough bibliography at the end. Every teacher ought to have this to pull out and read to or recite with students when time permits.

Snyder, Zilpha Keatley. **Song of the Gargoyle**. This is high adventure set in the Middle Ages. *See* SOCIAL STUDIES—ANCIENT AND EARLY CULTURES.

Speare, Elizabeth George. **The Sign of the Beaver**. A young boy learns to depend on the wisdom and knowledge of a Native American boy in order to survive in the wilderness. *See* SCIENCE.

Steinbeck, John. **The Red Pony**. Illus. Wesley Dennis. This is the classic story of a boy and his love for his pony. *See* ENGLISH—CLASSICS.

White, Robb. **The Lion's Paw**. Chuluota, FL: The Mickler House Publishers, 1983. 243p. $13.00. ISBN 0-913122-41-6.

Penny and Nick are orphans housed in an *eganahpro*, the word *orphanage* as seen from the inside of the gate. As "eganaps" in Florida in the 1940s, life was miserable and lonely, so they run away and meet up with an equally lonely boy, Ben, whose father is missing in action after World War II. His uncle, with whom he lives, is about to sell the sailboat he and his father built, much against Ben's will. Ben, Penny, and Nick set off in the sailboat, *The Lion's Paw*, to escape from the "eganahpro" people and Ben's uncle. They begin on the eastern side of Florida and sail through a series of canals, rivers, and lakes to get to the western shore and Captiva Island. Ben and his father are shell collectors and they need a Lion's Paw shell to complete their collections. Ben is sure that if they get to Captiva Island and find a Lion's Paw, his father will come home, and all will be well. They are pursued at every mile along the way, have many exciting adventures, and in true childlike behavior make many mistakes and have several close calls. This story was originally published in 1946 and contains some biased remarks about Japanese that need to be discussed. The story is sure to capture the listeners' attention as they follow the children's hair-raising adventures sailing across Florida.

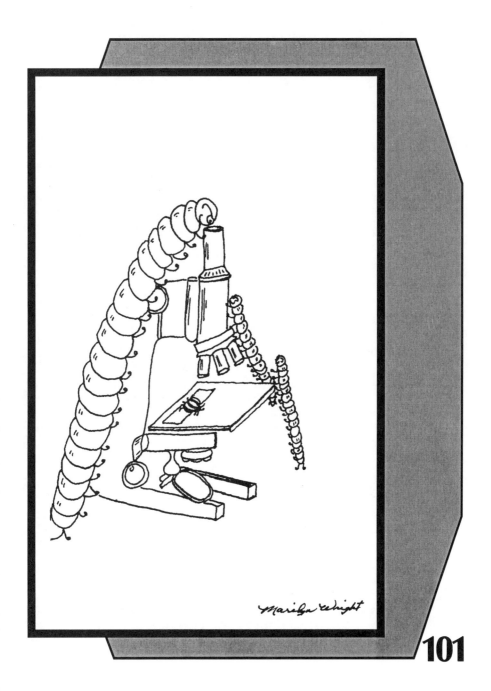

The books listed in this section are varied and include nonfiction books that combine science with other curricula, works of fiction that involve the need of scientific knowledge for survival and know-how, fantasy books that are based on scientific facts and theories, and others that celebrate the beauty of the natural world and its many wonders through prose and poetry.

Ames, Mildred. **Anna to the Infinite Power**. New York: Charles Scribner's Sons, 1981. 198p. $13.00. ISBN 0-684-16855-3.

When this book was written, the premise was treated as science fiction with some far-out ideas, but with recent scientific developments, the subject matter is quite timely. Anna is an unusual girl who excels in many things, but she's unemotional and lacks feeling, making her quite odd and difficult to understand. However, strange things are beginning to happen to her body and her mind, and she's beginning to be emotional and to care about people, especially her younger brother, Rowan. For the first time she is doing poorly in school, and she refuses to play the piano and study the subjects she's told to study. Her doctor, who has finally explained to her that she had "strange beginnings," sends her to a government research center on an island for observation. She secretly meets another "Anna," and they discover they are a part of the same cloning experiment that suddenly has begun to fail. Rather than all stay the same perfect clones, each Anna has begun to individualize; that is, to become her own person. Anna is overjoyed, but the doctors are horrified. Rowan realizes they intend to destroy the Annas because the experiment has gone awry and sneaks onto the island to free his sister. This science-fiction idea of cloning has actually become fact and encompasses genetic engineering, a topic currently discussed in science curricula.

Beshore, George. **Science in Ancient China**. New York: Franklin Watts, 1988. 95p. (Science in . . . Series). $10.50. ISBN 0-531-10485-0.

The Chinese had well-developed technology when Marco Polo visited in 1275, and he was amazed at the inventions they had compared with his native Italy. He found paved highways, rockets, movable type, and the compass. This book traces the development of ancient Chinese technology and scientific discoveries based on artifacts, written recordings, legends, and what Western explorers found when they traveled to China. The scientific developments are discussed along with the history of China, which makes this a valuable resource when studying ancient China. Many black-and-white photographs, drawings, and sketches help to present the information. A glossary, a bibliography for further readings, and an index are included. This is part of a series that is designed to share scientific and technological achievements of other cultures in other times.

————. **Science in Early Islamic Culture**. New York: Franklin Watts, 1988. 69p. (Science in . . . Series). $10.50. ISBN 0-531-10596-2.
Mohammed had his vision in a cave near Mecca around A.D. 610 telling him to begin a new religion that would unite people around the world. He did just that, sending vast armies to far lands and eventually ruling from the Atlantic Ocean in the west to India in the east. Along with this new religion, Islam, came centers of learning where scientific information known to a particular area was collected. They gathered and used scientific ideas from the Greeks, Egyptians, ancient Persians, and all other areas they controlled, therefore spreading and sharing knowledge among cultures. They also used experimentation, observation, and careful measurement of natural phenomena rather than the older method of simply speculating about the nature of things, thereby adding to scientific discoveries. This book discusses the important developments made during Islamic dominance from the eighth to the thirteenth century. Number systems, trigonometry, astronomy, engineering advancements, maps, and knowledge of the human body were among some of the ideas explored, developed, and used during this time. This book is an outstanding tool to use when studying the Islamic culture. A glossary, a bibliography, and an index are included. This is part of a series of books designed to explore scientific and technological achievements of ancient peoples.

Cooney, Miriam P., ed. **Celebrating Women in Mathematics and Science**. Short biographies of important women in mathematics and science are presented in short but informative chapters. *See* MATHEMATICS.

DeFelice, Cynthia. **The Apprenticeship of Lucas Whitaker**. New York: Farrar, Straus & Giroux, 1996. 151p. $15.00. ISBN 0-374-34669-0.
After everyone in Lucas Whitaker's family dies from consumption, he wanders off the farm and ends up in Southwick, Connecticut, where he takes a job as an apprentice to Doc Beecher. The doctor is kind and understanding, and Lucas and the doctor are concerned with the outbreak that is killing so many in the community. The doctor is convinced there must be a scientific, logical cause for the disease, which, if known, would lead to a cure. He purchases a new tool, a microscope, to probe and explore and try to come up with an answer. At the same time, out of desperation, the townspeople are practicing the "cure," a macabre ritual of digging up the remains of the first one in a family to contract the disease and burning the heart. The family member ill at the time breathes in the smoke from the burning heart, thus causing a cure. Lucas is torn between the beliefs of the townspeople and the doctor, who strongly opposes the

cure. So the wise doctor sends him to spend time with Moll, an old woman who lives on the outskirts of town who uses herbs for her healing powers. She soothes Lucas's body and spirit, helping him to grieve over the loss of his family and to sort out what could really be done for those who are ill. This book points out how desperate people were for answers before the days of modern medicine, and it reminds us of the great advances made in the medical field over the last 150 years. This is an excellent source to use when doing a health or disease unit and when studying United States history.

Demi. **Demi's Secret Garden**. This is a collection of beautifully illustrated poems about 19 different insects. *See* POETRY.

Drew, Helen. **My First Music Book**. This book contains step-by-step directions for making musical instruments to demonstrate sound. *See* FINE ARTS.

Gay, Kathlyn. **Science in Ancient Greece**. New York: Franklin Watts, 1988. 95p. (Science in . . . Series). $10.50. ISBN 0-531-10487-7.
    It seems paradoxical that science blossomed in the ancient Greek civilization considering how strongly the Greeks believed that the gods had absolute power and dominion over nature and people. However, historians believe the thirst for knowledge began with even earlier civilizations, setting the stage for scientific advancements during the Greek era. The Greek philosopher-scientists differed from other civilizations because they gathered factual information, developed theories, and recorded information, but they didn't necessarily test and experiment. Therefore, science and philosophy went hand in hand, because much of their scientific information was actually theory and philosophy. This book, a part of a series designed to highlight scientific and technological achievements during early cultures, explains the many advancements during the time of the ancient Greeks. Theories about creation, astronomy, atoms, the planets, mathematics, geography, the human body, engineering, and building were advanced. The work of Pythagoras, Hippocrates, Apollonius, Euclid, Aristarchus, Hipparchus, Ptolemy, Anaximander, Hecataeus, Eratosthenes, Galen, Aristotle, Theophrastus, Socrates, Plato, Archimedes, Ctesibius, and others is discussed. Photographs, drawings, and sketches as well as the glossary, bibliography, and index, make this an important tool when studying ancient Greece.

George, Jean Craighead. **Julie of the Wolves**. Illus. John Schoenherr. New York: Harper & Row, 1972. 170p. $15.00. ISBN 0-06-021944-0, 0-440-84444-4pa.
    When Miyax's Eskimo father, Kapugen, fails to return from a hunting trip, she is sent to live with the man she was promised to as a baby only to discover that Daniel is retarded and can't possibly be her husband. She decides to run away to San Francisco to live with her pen

pal who knows her by her American name, Julie. She leaves hurriedly, taking only a few items with her that she thinks she'll need in California. However, it's summer with sun nearly all the time, and she becomes confused and ends up lost on the North Slope of Alaska with no food and few survival tools. Using her extensive knowledge of the arctic wilderness that she learned from her father, she fashions a home, sewing tools, and cooking utensils. However, she needs meat, and the only way to get that is by befriending the wolves. So she behaves like a young pup, and after much patience is accepted by a wolf pack and survives. Jean Craighead George's extensive knowledge of the outdoors is exhibited in this work in which she describes in detail the habits and ways of the wolves and their ability to survive. She also points out the vulnerability of the wolves because of hunters shooting from airplanes. Julie is a part of both modern-day Alaska and the old Eskimo ways, and she is torn between the two when they clash. This is a marvelous survival story that uses scientific knowledge to solve problems. In the sequel, *Julie*, she continues her saga and her quest to save the wolves. A third book, *Julie's Wolf Pack*, in which Kapu, Amaroq's son, becomes the leader of the wolf pack, has recently been released.

————. **My Side of the Mountain**. New York: Dutton Children's Books, 1988, originally released in 1959. 177p. $14.00. ISBN 0-525-44392-4.

Sam Gribley leads an okay life, but he's tired of living in cramped quarters in the city. So he does what so many people would like to do: He runs away to live in the country. He sets up housekeeping in the Catskill Mountains on some property owned by his grandfather in a huge hollow tree that becomes his home. The animals and plants in the woods and the fish in the stream provide his food, he makes clothes from animal skins, and he trains a falcon to help hunt food for him. Sam manages to survive storms and all kinds of weather, and when he needs information, he walks to the nearest town and uses the library. He loves his life, but when summer arrives, so do hikers, other campers, and finally, his entire family. Jean Craighead George is a naturalist who expresses her love of nature by writing children's literature about it. What Sam does and what he eats are based on factual information based on her experiences and study. This book earned the Newbery Honor Award. Sam's many adventures make this a great read aloud.

————. **On the Far Side of the Mountain**. New York: Dutton Children's Books, 1990. 170p. $13.95. ISBN 0-525-44563-3 (trade), 0-14-034248-6pa.

Writing a sequel to a successful book such as *My Side of the Mountain* is risky, but Jean Craighead George does a masterful job of continuing Sam Gribley's quest to live in the wilds with only nature to surround him. His peaceful way of life is disturbed when a conservation officer comes to take his peregrine falcon, Faithful, away from him because it's against the law to keep peregrine falcons unless licensed. His privacy is further disrupted when his sister, Alice, comes to live with him. He must provide food for himself and Alice without Faithful to hunt for him, and he must satisfy Alice's many demands. She wants to live in the country, but she wants all the comforts of home, including electricity. Sam's life is changed, and with Alice come many adventures, but Sam never gives up on his dream to live in the wilds. This sequel also makes a great read aloud.

Harris, Robie H. **It's Perfectly Normal: Changing Bodies, Growing Up, Sex and Sexual Health**. Illus. Michael Emberley. Cambridge, MA: Candlewick Press, 1994. 89p. $19.95. ISBN 1-56402-199-8, 1-56402-159-9pa.
>   Two cartoon characters, a curious bird and a squeamish bee, help to present honest, open information on sexuality. The information is divided into six main sections: "What Is Sex," "Our Bodies," "Puberty, Families and Babies," "Decisions," and "Staying Healthy." Within these six sections nearly every aspect of sexuality is discussed in an open, frank, and thorough, yet tasteful, presentation. The illustrations are scientifically correct but are done in a light, humorous manner, which fits the text perfectly. This is the most informative and tastefully done book about teenage sexuality on the market at this time.

Hinshaw, Dorothy. **Quetzal, Sacred Bird of the Cloud Forest**. Fact and fiction about the Quetzal bird of Central America is presented in this unique book. *See* SOCIAL STUDIES—ANCIENT AND EARLY CULTURES.

Hobbs, Will. **Bearstone**. A troubled Navajo boy gets in touch with himself with the help of an old man, nature, and the outdoors. *See* ENGLISH—CLASSICS.

————. **Downriver**. New York: Atheneum, 1991. 204p. $15.00. ISBN 0-689-31690-9, 0-553-29717-1pa.
>   Discovery Unlimited, better known as Hoods in the Woods by the troubled teenagers involved in the program, is a program that challenges teens and gives them self-esteem by conquering the outdoors. This particular group has many unhappy campers, and they refuse to obey the leader, Al. The kids decide they want to raft the Grand Canyon rather than the tamer and safer San Juan River. The group takes off with the van and the trailer while Al is getting a permit, thus beginning the high adventure of whitewater rafting the Grand Canyon without a leader and without maps. There are few dull moments while this crazy group of careless and unskilled kids rafts one of the most difficult waterways in the country. Hobbs's own outdoor experiences give him expertise in this adventure, making it scientifically accurate as well as exciting. A sequel, *River Thunder*, has recently been released.

————. **Far North**. New York: Morrow Junior Books, 1996. 226p. $15.00. ISBN 0-688-14192-7.

The setting for this suspenseful outdoor adventure is the Nahanni River area of the Northwest Territory of Canada. After their floatplane is lost, the passengers Gabe and Raymond, roommates at a boarding school, and Raymond's distant relative, Johnny, an elderly and ill Native American who grew up in this area, are stranded in the remote part of Canada in the midst of winter. They have few supplies and even less food, so their survival depends on Johnny's extensive knowledge of the wilderness and their own common sense, sometimes sorely lacking. Their adventures are realistic and dramatic, making this is a real page-turner that is sure to keep the reader involved. Readers will enjoy knowing that Hobbs was inspired to write this story after traveling to the area and rafting and canoeing down the river. He studied the writings of others who had experienced this harsh land, especially R. M. Patterson, whose cabin is a part of this book.

————. **Ghost Canoe**. A young boy sets out to solve the mystery of a shipwreck off the Northwest coast in the 1800s. *See* GREATEST OF THE LATEST.

Klass, David. **California Blue**. New York: Scholastic, 1994. 199p. $13.95. ISBN 0-590-46688-7, 0-590-46689-5pa.

This gripping story, set in the redwoods of Northern California, is told by John Rodgers, whose father works at the local lumber mill, as do most of the people in town. The mill owners are intent on lumbering a section of old-growth redwoods, an act that is strongly opposed by environmentalists. John has a tough time with the mill's decision because he loves running through the redwoods, yet he understands how important the trees are to the livelihood of the townspeople. To further complicate the issue, he discovers a nearly extinct type of butterfly living in the old-growth trees, and he knows that if government officials find out about the butterfly, the mill will be unable to cut the trees, which will please the environmentalists but probably cause the mill to close. He finally reveals his dilemma to his science teacher, Miss Merrill, who suggests they contact her professor from Berkeley, Dr. Eggleson, who she feels will give them good advice about how to handle the situation. Dr. Eggleson arrives and promises to hold all information in deepest confidence, but John soon discovers to his horror that Dr. Eggleson is using this cause to further his own reputation and blows the situation wide-open. Klass has done a magnificent job of bringing validity to both sides of the issue and causes the reader to realize that no issue has clear-cut right or wrong answers. This is a passionate and gripping novel that brings out emotion and empathy for all involved. It is an excellent novel to use when discussing environmental concerns or when dealing with decision making.

Lasky, Kathryn. **The Librarian Who Measured the Earth**. The accomplishments of Eratosthenes, the Greek scientist, mathematician, author, and geographer, are told in a delightful and informative picture-book format. *See* MATHEMATICS.

Moss, Carol. **Science in Ancient Mesopotamia**. New York: Franklin Watts, 1988. 71p. (Science in . . . Series) $10.50. ISBN 0-531-10594-6.

 The world's oldest civilization, Mesopotamia, was also the birthplace of early science and technology. The people were busy creating settlements and cities, which set the stage for learning and discovery, and with their industrious and creative powers they made scientific discoveries and recorded them. Even more importantly, this early civilization helped build a foundation in science that would be used in the following centuries. This book, one in a series that deals with scientific and technological achievements of early cultures, gathers together the scientific accomplishments of the Sumerians and Babylonians from 3500 B.C. to about 100 B.C. and relates the importance of these accomplishments to today's world. The development of writing was of great importance, as was information about diseases, the human body, drugs and medicines, and surgery. They invented the base ten number system and the idea of zero as well as the idea of fractions, weights, and measurements. Developments in astronomy, a calendar, and the observation of things in nature—including plants, animals, rocks, and minerals—were among their accomplishments, and they learned to use their immediate surroundings to advance their culture by developing irrigation. They learned to use clay to write on and as a building material and learned to make glass and to mix metals together to make alloys. A glossary, a bibliography, and an index are included.

North, Sterling. **Rascal: A Memoir of a Better Era**. Illus. John Schoenherr. New York: E. P. Dutton, 1963, reissued in 1984. 189p. $13.00. ISBN 0-525-18839-8.

 Sterling North grew up in southern Wisconsin during World War I. His mother had died, his older brother was fighting in the war, and his sister lived in another city. So he and his father lived a rather carefree life running their household as they pleased. Sterling loved animals and brought many of them home with him, but his favorite was a raccoon named Rascal, who was allowed free run of the house. This is the true story of Sterling and Rascal and their many experiences together—most of them humorous. They roamed the woods, went fishing and camping, and spent endless hours together. However, Rascal lived up to his name and often harassed the neighbors, so Sterling had to build a pen for him. As Rascal grew up, Sterling realized that even though they were dearest friends, if he truly loved Rascal, he would have to let him go into the wild to join other raccoons. This funny yet touching story includes a great deal of scientific information as well as a strong reverence and respect for nature. It makes a terrific read aloud because of Rascal's hilarious antics.

O'Dell, Scott. **Streams to the River, River to the Sea: A Novel of Saca-gawea**. Lewis and Clark kept careful records about the plants, animals, bodies of water, and their environment on their 4,000-mile journey to the Pacific Ocean. This account describes what the environment of the United States was like before it was settled. *See* SOCIAL STUDIES—UNITED STATES HISTORY.

Paulsen, Gary. **Brian's Winter**. New York: Delacorte Press, 1996. 133p. $15.95. ISBN 0-385-32198-8.

    Every *Hatchet* (Paulsen, 1987) and *River* (Paulsen, 1991) fan will be eager to read this latest survival adventure about Brian. In *Hatchet*, the small plane in which Brian is flying crashes, the pilot dies, and Brian is left to survive on his own in the wilds of Canada until he is rescued. In *River*, Brian returns to Canada to re-create the experience, this time fully outfitted and monitored by National Geographic. *Brian's Winter* assumes Brian is not rescued at the end of *Hatchet*, and he needs to learn winter survival. Brian's survival depends on his knowledge of the weather, the animal's winter habits, the trees, and the area in which he finds himself. This is a fast-paced, exciting book jam-packed with infor-mation about the arctic winter environment.

———. **Hatchet**. New York: Bradbury Press, 1987. 142p. $12.95. ISBN 0-02-77-130-1.

    Brian's mother gives him a new hatchet as he boards the small plane bound for Canada where he'll be spending the summer with his father, camping and enjoying other outdoor activities. But the pilot suffers a fatal heart attack, and Brian is left stranded aloft in the plane. It crashes into a lake after flying uncontrolled for quite some time, veering off course, and making it impossible for rescuers to find it. Brian finds himself in the wilds of Canada with nothing but a hatchet because his gear is in the plane at the bottom of the lake. To survive, he needs shelter, food, and a way to survive the insects. He uses his knowledge of nature, which he learned by camping with his father, but he also learns by observing, and by trial and error and logical thinking. He has one adven-ture after another with the weather, insects, food sources, and wild animals, and though he begins to feel at home, he knows winter is coming and he'll need more clothing, food, and better shelter to survive. He forces himself to dive into the plane to retrieve what he can and discovers the plane's transmitter is still working. He begins sending signals that are picked up by another plane that eventually takes Brian to safety. This exciting adventure hooks readers and holds their interest. It's excellent for reluctant readers because the subject matter is so compelling, and it makes a great read aloud. There are two sequels, *River*, in which Brian goes back to reenact the episode for National Geographic, and *Brian's Winter* which assumes Brian lives in his shelter during the winter.

Ride, Sally, and Tam O'Shaughnessy. **The Third Planet: Exploring the Earth from Space**. New York: Crown, 1994. 46p. ISBN 0-517-59361-0 (trade), 0-517-59362-9 (lib. bdg.).

In 1983 Sally Ride became the first woman to go into space on the spaceship *Challenger*, and in this book she tells the story of Earth, the third planet, using the photographs she took while in orbit. Every page is jammed with outstanding photographs of the Earth that are set on a black background, giving them a striking appearance. Information about the Earth and its atmosphere, ozone layer, orbit, oceans, weather, living things, greenhouse effect, and its ever-changing appearance is sandwiched between the abundant photographs. This is a marvelous sourcebook for the study of the planet Earth as well as space travel, or it may simply be enjoyed as a photographic essay.

Ryder, Joanne. **Jaguar in the Rain Forest**. Illus. Michael Rothman. New York: Morrow Junior Books, 1996. 32p. (Just for a Day). $16.00. ISBN 0-688-12990-0 (trade), 0-688-12991-9 (lib. bdg.).

When studying animals, specifically jaguars, or the rain forest, you will definitely want to use this book. Every inch of the large two-page spreads is filled with action and color, illustrating the jaguar's actions in the rain forest. By telling the jaguar's story, information is given about other animals in the rain forest as well. The pages are so colorful and action packed, it's easy to imagine you are right there in the forest. The text describes the adventure, but the best scientific information can be found in the author's notes at the beginning of the book.

———. **Shark in the Sea**. Illus. Michael Rothman. New York: Morrow Junior Books, 1997. Unpaged. (Just for a Day). $16.00. ISBN 0-688-1409-X (trade), 0-688-14910-3 (lib. bdg.).

If you need beautiful illustrations of sharks and their habits and habitats, this is just the book for you. Each two-page spread is filled with large paintings of sharks, showing their bodies from different views depending on which way the shark is turned. The text is minimal but describes what is happening on each page. The author's notes at the beginning of the book give several paragraphs of good, concise scientific information, and the outstanding paintings of sharks will be invaluable to anyone interested in this topic.

Schertle, Alice. **Advice for a Frog**. Illus. Norman Green. New York: Lothrop, Lee & Shepard, 1995. 30p. $16.00. ISBN 0-688-13486-6 (trade), 0-688-13487-4 (lib. bdg.).

Science and language combine beautifully in this outstanding collection of poetry featuring 14 animals, including the toucan, fruit bat, pangolin, crowned crane, frilled lizard, harpy eagle, cheetah, brown rat, Galápagos tortoise, black rhino, king vulture, iguana, proboscis monkey, and the secretary bird. Each brightly colored two-page spread includes a thought-provoking poem about the animal and is surrounded with a superb illustration. The illustrations are so remarkable, they would make fabulous posters for decorative purposes. An informational paragraph about each animal is included at the end of the book. This would tie in well with environmental studies or when studying animals and birds.

Siebert, Diane. **Sierra**. Illus. Wendell Minor. New York: HarperCollins, 1991. Unpaged. $14.95. ISBN 0-06021639-5 (trade), 0-06-021640-9 (lib. bdg.).

The majesty and mysticism of the Sierra Nevada is captured in the poem told by one of the mountains. It gives the geological history of the mountain range and tells about the giant redwoods, the delicate plants and multitude of animals, the winds and the weather, the seasons, and the timelessness and power of the mountains. The beautiful words are augmented and enhanced with majestic, realistic, descriptive illustrations that beautifully convey the feeling of the poem. This work of art will be well received by science and literature students.

Sis, Peter. **Starry Messenger: A Book Depicting the Life of a Famous Scientist, Mathematician, Astronomer, Philosopher and Physicist, Galileo Galilei**. New York: Frances Foster Books, Farrar, Straus & Giroux, 1996. 33p. $16.00. ISBN 0-374-37191-1.

Every page of this oversize book is jammed with tidbits of information about Galileo and his times. It gives an excellent biography of Galileo, his struggles with society and religion at that time, and his marvelous scientific achievements. The illustrations are large and colorful and filled with drawings and symbols depicting the text. To add information, each two-page spread has a handwritten insert inscribed in a unique manner. Some are curled around and around, some are written sideways, and others label items in the illustrations or are written in boxes. Be prepared to spend a great deal of time examining every detail in this exceptional book.

Speare, Elizabeth George. **The Sign of the Beaver**. Boston: Houghton Mifflin, 1983. 135p. $8.95. ISBN 0-395-33890-5, 0-440-77903-0pa.

In the 1700s, when the majority of the country was unsettled by White men, Matt's father decides it's becoming too crowded in Massachusetts and stakes claim to a new life in Maine territory. Matt and his father clear an area, build a log cabin, and plant a garden. Father then returns to Massachusetts to fetch Matt's mother, sister, and the new baby that was to be born while they were gone. Matt notches a stick every day to count the six weeks his father said it would take before his return. While he waits, Matt learns many hard lessons about life in the wilderness from a Native American boy who saves Matt's life when he is nearly killed by swarms of bees. The boy shows Matt how to hunt without a gun, how to fish without fish hooks, how to save himself from an attack by a bear, and many other life-saving techniques. Many weeks pass, but his family doesn't arrive. With winter coming, Matt makes the big decision whether to continue living in Maine or to travel back to

Massachusetts before the harsh weather sets in, which would mean he didn't really trust his father's word. He decides to stay, and his family does finally arrive, but only after Matt learns important lessons about wilderness survival and gains respect for the Native Americans. Matt's many adventures make this an excellent read aloud, and it's also a useful source when studying the early United States.

Wiesner, David. **June 29, 1999**. New York: Clarion Books, 1992. 32p. $15.99. ISBN 0-395-59762-5.

This hilarious picture book about a science experiment presumably gone wrong is good for students who are beginning science experiments. On May 11, 1999, Holly Evans launches vegetable seedlings into the sky in little, well-marked boxes, each carried by a weather balloon. She presents the experiment to her class and explains that she intends to study the effects of extraterrestrial conditions on vegetable growth and development. Soon after her launch, massive vegetables begin to rain down places all over Earth. David Wiesner's illustrations of the enormous cabbages, artichokes, turnips, and other vegetables descending on towns and people are terrific. Holly is horrified thinking the vegetables are a result of her experiment gone awry until she realizes that some of the vegetables were not included in her experiment. The reader discovers that a star cruiser from Arcturia has accidentally spilled its food supply just as it was passing the "small blue planet." The creatures are despondent, wondering where their next meal will come from, when in wander little boxes—carried by orange weather balloons—with vegetables growing in them.

Woods, Geraldine. **Science in Ancient Egypt**. New York: Franklin Watts, 1988. 92p. (Science in . . . Series). $10.50. ISBN 0-531-10486-9.

The ancient Egyptians led a rather peaceful existence, which gave them time to develop art, design, crafts, science, and technology. This book, one in a series designed to highlight scientific and technological achievements of ancient and early cultures, examines the many achievements of the Egyptians in geography, science, building, mathematics, astronomy, medicine, writing, irrigation, agriculture, and other crafts and technology that relate to our present-day society. Their construction of the pyramids was a monumental feat, but it couldn't have been done without some other advancements made during this time, such as a system of counting, mathematical symbols, measurement, and figuring areas and angles. Egyptians' study of astronomy was advanced along with the development of clocks, and timekeeping and mummification could not have taken place without their study of the human body. The Egyptians also advanced the idea of symbols and writing along with writing tools, and pottery, clay, glass, faience, metals and metalwork, stonework, woodwork, paints, glues, weaving, and boatbuilding were discovered, developed, and used by the Egyptians. Photographs, drawings, and sketches along with a glossary, a bibliography, and an index make this an excellent source when studying ancient Egypt.

Chapter 13
SOCIAL STUDIES— UNITED STATES HISTORY

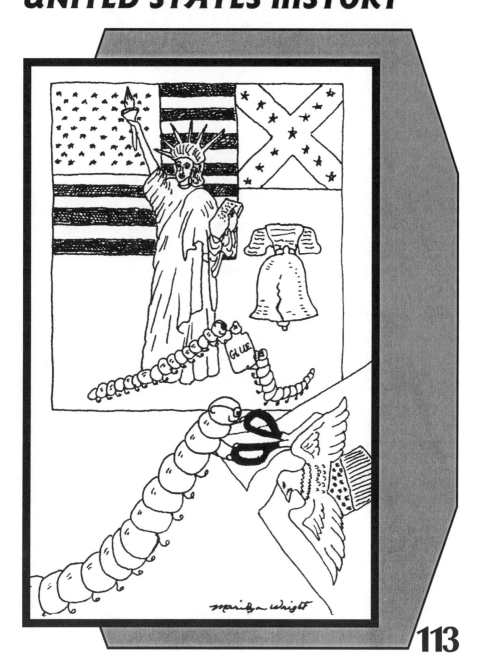

Much can be learned about the history of the United States through historical fiction novels for children that are often well researched and written with great care and accuracy. History will come alive through the characters presented in these books, which span the history of the United States from earliest settlement to the present.

Avi. **Beyond the Western Sea: Book One, Escape from Home**. New York: Orchard, 1996. 295p. $18.95. ISBN 0-531-09513-4 (trade), 0-531-08863-4 (lib. bdg.).

In the first of two books, Avi takes us to Ireland in 1850, when the masses are starving and often homeless. The O'Connell family have just been evicted from their meager home, so Laura, Patrick, and their mother head to Liverpool, to embark for America to meet up with their father. They immediately encounter swindlers, adventurers, an actor, a runaway aristocratic young boy, and a host of wild escapades. Each short chapter ends on a mysterious note, compelling the reader to quickly discover what happens next. Avi exposes us to life as it was in Ireland and England in the 1850s and gives an excellent background on the mass migration of Europeans to the United States during this time period.

————. **Beyond the Western Sea: Book Two, Lord Kirkle's Money**. New York: Orchard, 1996. 380p. $18.95. ISBN 0-531-09520-79 (trade), 0-531-08870-7 (lib. bdg.).

Book Two involves the same cast of characters as Book One, but this time they're on board a ship headed to America. Sir Laurence, the aristocratic runaway is now a stowaway, and Laura and Patrick continue to have one adventure after the next. They make it to America, only to discover their father has died because of the difficult conditions in the textile mills, but the plucky kids land on their feet, finding a place to live and getting jobs. Through the children's adventures the reader learns a great deal about European immigration, life in America during the Industrial Age, and the attitude toward immigrants at that time.

————. **The Fighting Ground**. Thirteen-year-old Jonathan runs off to join the Revolutionary War and over the next 24 hours comes to terms with the realities of war. The story is divided by the minutes of the day rather than by chapters. *See* UNIQUE PRESENTATIONS.

————. **Nothing but the Truth**. A student is suspended for singing along with the "National Anthem." *See* UNIQUE PRESENTATIONS.

————. **The True Confessions of Charlotte Doyle**. A 13-year-old girl, Charlotte, is the only female on a ship traveling from Liverpool, England, to Providence, Rhode Island, in 1832. The crew mutinies, and she is caught up in danger, mystery, and intrigue. Life at this time is well-portrayed—especially for women in society. *See* ENGLISH— CLASSICS.

————. **"Who Was That Masked Man, Anyway?"** Life in 1945 in the United States is portrayed in this story about Frankie and Mario, who are hooked on radio programs and will go to any length to listen to their favorite shows. World War II is just ending and Frankie's wounded brother, Tom, has just returned home. The entire story is told through dialogue. *See* UNIQUE PRESENTATIONS.

Bial, Raymond. **The Underground Railroad**. Boston: Houghton Mifflin, 1995. 48p. $14.00. ISBN 0-395-69937-1.

> One of the most interesting chapters in American history is the saga of the Underground Railroad. Much has been written about it, but this book is unique because the author visited the actual "stations," slave quarters, and places where important events dealing with slavery and the Underground Railroad took place. He took photographs in black and white and in color to best portray the feeling and spirit of the Underground Railroad and captured the importance of the movement by photographing many houses, churches, barns and other places that housed "passengers." One particularly interesting photograph is of a slave's wooden shoe with a big hole on the sole. He also includes several copies of wanted posters, sketches of an auction block where slaves were bought and sold, and a map showing the Underground Railroad routes in 1860. The text is well organized, easy to read, yet detailed and informational. A chronology of the antislavery movement in America, a bibliography, and an index are included. This is the type of book that is great for research but also interesting to read because of the subject.

Blos, Joan W. **A Gathering of Days: A New England Girl's Journal, 1830–32**. With diary entries, Catherine Hall tells the story of life on a small New Hampshire farm in the 1830s. She tells about life without her mother, taking care of the household and her little sister, her father's remarriage, and everyday life, including quilting, berrying, sugaring, death, and romance. *See* UNIQUE PRESENTATIONS.

Bolotin, Norman, and Angela Herb. **For Home and Country: A Civil War Scrapbook**. New York: Lodestar Books, 1995. 98p. $15.00. ISBN 0-525-67495-0, 0-590-99736-Xpa.

> The use of primary sources is often the best method when teaching about a particular time period. This work—considered one of the top primary sourcebooks on the Civil War—gathers together a staggering amount of photographs, newspaper and magazine articles, personal letters, sketches and drawings, posters, accounting sheets, advertisements, maps, songs, and other memorabilia to tell the story of that war. It begins with a detailed time line that clearly shows the main events of the war and sets the stage for the impressive amount of information presented in the following chapters. A glossary, a bibliography, and an index of picture credits are included.

Bray, Rosemary. **Martin Luther King**. This biography of Martin Luther King Jr. is in picture-book format with extended text. *See* BIOGRAPHIES.

Bunting, Eve. **Dandelions**. Illus. Greg Shed. New York: Harcourt Brace & Company, 1995. 48p. $15.00. ISBN 0-15-200050-X.

> The westward movement is vividly portrayed in this beautifully illustrated picture book. Papa is overjoyed to be moving from Illinois to the Nebraska Territory, but Mama, who is pregnant, has trouble sharing his enthusiasm. The journey is long and arduous, but they finally make it to a land with nothing but grass. Once there, Papa enthusiastically digs a well and builds a sod house. However, Mama is still melancholy and silent, which bothers the two girls, Zoe and Rebecca. Zoe, the oldest daughter and narrator of the story, accompanies Papa into town for supplies, and she and Papa look for a special birthday gift for Mama. Zoe spots a dandelion plant, which they dig up to take to Mama, hoping it will remind her of Illinois. They plant it on the roof of the sod house, much to Mama's delight. The story is tender and touching, expressing the emotions felt by so many women who were transplanted to a hostile land against their wishes. The illustrations, done in earthy tones, give the feeling of actually being there on the plains.

Collier, James Lincoln, and Christopher Collier. **My Brother Sam Is Dead**. New York: Four Winds Press, 1985. 216p. $12.00. ISBN 0-02-722980-7, 0-590-42792-Xpa.

> From the beginning of the book it is known that Tim Meeker's older brother, Sam, has died, but what isn't known are the circumstances surrounding his death. These are revealed little by little as the story is told. Mr. Meeker, an innkeeper in Connecticut, tries hard to remain neutral—siding neither with the British nor the revolutionaries—but his son, Sam, runs off to fight with the revolutionaries. As the war rages on, soldiers on both sides need food and forage throughout the countryside, taking whatever they can find to eat. Sam becomes involved in a

food raid, causing him to be imprisoned. Meanwhile, Tim and his father have trouble getting food and ale to serve at the inn, so they take the wagon and oxen on a daring journey to stock the inn for the winter. Tim is brave and manages to talk himself out of trouble when accosted by rustlers, but his father is taken away and later killed. Tim and his mother are left to carry on all the work, which fouls up Tim's plan of joining the army. Sam is killed by the revolutionary officers for cattle rustling, and his mother and Tim continue with the inn until the end of the war. The Revolutionary War was highly emotional and caused great grief and harm to the common man, as can be seen by this account. The Collier brothers are expert historians and do extensive research, making all their books historically accurate.

Conrad, Pam. **Prairie Songs**. Illus. Darryl S. Zudeck. New York: Harper & Row, 1985. 167p. $14.00. ISBN 0-06-021336-1 (trade), 0-06-021337-X (lib. bdg.), 0-06-440206-1pa.

Some people thrived on the prairie during the time when it was being settled; others simply couldn't handle it. Louisa loves the Nebraska prairie, having grown up there. A young doctor and his wife move there, much to the satisfaction of the community. Louisa loves it because the doctor's wife, Emmeline, is beautiful and delicate, gives her and her brother reading lessons, and reads poetry to them. The doctor loves the country and thrives, but Emmeline, who is pregnant, hates it more every day. She loses the baby, goes mad, and dies. The experience is alarming to Louisa but teaches her once again that the prairie isn't for everyone. Wound into the story is a substory about a real photographer, Samuel Butcher, who traveled throughout the prairie taking pictures of the homesteaders. The families treasured these photographs, but more importantly, Butcher kept albums of these photographs, which have become an important tool for chronicling this time period. This moving story is an excellent source to use in conjunction with the study of the westward movement and would be effective used along with *Dandelions*, by Eve Bunting.

Curtis, Christopher. **The Watsons Go to Birmingham—1963**. New York: Delacorte Press, 1995. 210p. $14.95. ISBN0-385-32175-9.

The Watsons, a Black couple living in Flint, Michigan, during the 1960s, are striving to do a good job of raising their three children, but the oldest son begins to have some behavioral problems. The parents decide it's time for him to spend the summer with Grandma in Birmingham. The parents plan the trip to Birmingham with great care and decide to make it a vacation to remember. The first Sunday they are in Birmingham, the little sister goes to Sunday school with some of Grandma's neighbors. It happens to be the day the five little girls are killed when their church is bombed. What begins as a somewhat lighthearted story ends up effectively telling an important piece of the Civil Right's movement. This is an outstanding work that won the Newbery Honor Award in 1996.

Cushman, Karen. **The Ballad of Lucy Whipple**. The story of the California gold rush is told through the eyes of a young girl. *See* GREATEST OF THE LATEST.

DeFelice, Cynthia. **The Apprenticeship of Lucas Whitaker**. In the mid-1800s the causes for diseases were not understood, and cures for life-threatening diseases often included magic and superstition rather than scientific reasoning. Lucas is apprenticed to a doctor who fights to save people from a tuberculosis outbreak. *See* SCIENCE.

————. **Weasel**. Weasel, an evil man who hunts people for the sport of it, captures and injures Nathan and Molly's father in the wilds of Ohio in 1839. Ezra, a large, shaggy-looking, speechless man helps save Father. *See* READ ALOUDS.

Everett, Gwen. **John Brown: One Man Against Slavery**. This biography of John Brown, done in picture-book format, is told from his daughter's perspective. *See* BIOGRAPHIES.

Fox, Paula. **The Slave Dancer**. Illus. Eros Keith. Scarsdale, NY: Bradbury Press, 1973. 176p. $14.00. ISBN 0-02-735560-8, 0-87888-062-3.
When Jessie Bollier's mother, a seamstress, sends him out to buy a spool of thread, she expects he will return within a few minutes rather than four long months later. In 1840, Jessie, age 13, lives with his mother and sister in New Orleans, earning a few pennies now and then by playing his fife on the docks. On the night his mother sends him out to buy thread, he is suddenly kidnapped and thrown onto a ship, *The Moonlight*. The ship sails to Africa, where Black slaves are loaded aboard, packed in the hold, and chained in place but given little food and only a half a cup of water per day. The ship is carrying the slaves illegally, so the destination is Cuba, not the United States. Jessie's job, whether he wants it or not, is to "dance" the slaves. Every other morning, groups of slaves, unclothed and filthy, are brought on deck and made to move to the sounds of Jessie's fife to give them exercise but also for the entertainment of the crew. Jessie is appalled by this activity but he is threatened with whippings if he doesn't do his job. As the voyage continues he witnesses amazing atrocities done to the crewmembers as well as to the captured slaves as ordered by the evil Captain Cawthorne. When the ship is close to Cuba, an American ship comes close, causing instant pandemonium, and all the Blacks are thrown overboard to prevent discovery of the illegal cargo. The ship is frantically sailed into a storm and wrecks. Jessie and Raz, a Black boy he protected, survive and manage to swim to land, which turns out to be Mississippi. He meets an old man, Daniel, who feeds them, finds safety for Raz, and directs Jessie toward his home. The story is often brutal, astonishing, and painful to read, but it is based on fact and tells the difficult story of slave trade as

seen from a young boy's eyes. This book won the Newbery Medal for its outstanding writing and should be included when studying slavery and the Civil War.

Fritz, Jean. **Harriet Beecher Stowe and the Beecher Preachers**. This is an outstanding biography of Harriet Beecher Stowe and the part she played in the Civil War. *See* BIOGRAPHIES.

Glass, Andrew. **The Sweetwater Run: The Story of Buffalo Bill Cody and the Pony Express**. New York: Doubleday Books for Young Readers, 1996. 41p. $15.95. ISBN 0-385-32220-8.

    The fascinating story of the Pony Express is told through the eyes of Will Cody, later known as Buffalo Bill Cody, when he is 13 years old. He wants to be a rider but is considered too young and too small, so he becomes a stable boy. One of the riders is bitten by a snake and unable to ride, but the mail with the presidential-election results has to go through. So Will jumps on the horse and successfully continues the journey. Through this fictionalized story we learn how the Pony Express operated, the many dangers encountered by the riders, and the intense zeal felt by everyone connected to the operation to get the mail through. The illustrations are colorful and a bit comical but clearly depict the action and intensity of the riders. The Pony Express route and all its stops are shown clearly on a map of the western United States. The last four pages of "Notes" give the factual story of the Pony Express and a biographical account of William Frederick Cody. For another account of the Pony Express, see the story by Cheryl Harness, *They're Off! The Story of the Pony Express.*

Harness, Cheryl. **They're Off! The Story of the Pony Express**. New York: Simon & Schuster Books for Young Readers, 1996. 32p. $16.00. ISBN 0-689-80523-3.

    One of the most exciting and intriguing stories in the development of the United States is the saga of the Pony Express. Along with the westward expansion came the desire to stay connected to families and friends, but it could take years for a letter to get from one end of the country to the other. The Butterfield Overland, a stagecoach company, was hired by the U.S. government to carry mail, but it only operated along the southern route, totally ignoring the central and northern parts of the country. In 1860, William H. Russell talked his business partners— Alexander Majors and William Bradford Waddell—into starting a new mail-delivery service with horseback riders rather than stagecoaches. They set up the company and had it operational in 65 days—a major feat. They hired "young, skinny wiry fellows, not over eighteen" for $25 per week to ride through rough terrain, endure nearly impossible weather, and encounter angry Native Americans. Despite these difficulties, they were able to carry the mail from San Francisco, California, to St. Joseph, Missouri, in as few as 10 days. The business partners put out hundreds of thousands of dollars but were never reimbursed by the federal government, and after 16 months the company folded due to lack of funding but also because telegraph wires were being installed, tying the country together in an even faster and certainly easier way. The illustrations depict the excitement of the time, and maps are included that show the routes followed. A list of the 182 Pony Express riders is given in the back of the book along with a bibliography. For a more fictionalized version of the Pony Express told through the eyes of Buffalo Bill Cody, see the story by Andrew Glass, *The Sweetwater Run: The Story of Buffalo Bill Cody and the Pony Express.*

Hobbs, Will. **Ghost Canoe**. A young boy attempts to solve the murder of the captain of a wrecked ship in the Northwest in the 1870s. *See* GREATEST OF THE LATEST.

Howard, Ellen. **The Log Cabin Quilt**. Illus. Ronald Himler. New York: Holiday House, 1996. 32p. $15.95. ISBN 0-8234-1247-4.

After Mam died, Pap, Granny, and the three children—Sis, Bub, and Elvirey—set out in a covered wagon from their comfortable home in Carolina to the unsettled woods of Michigan. This is Pap's idea, and everyone else has no choice but to go along with it. After reaching Michigan, they build a log cabin and put all their belongings into it, but it still doesn't feel like home because Mam is not there. No one speaks her name, but everyone is grieving in their own way. When the first big storm arrives, Pap is out hunting, and the others are left alone, worrying about Pap and trying to stay warm. They discover that the chinking in the log cabin has frozen, causing it to contract and allowing the cold to pour through. Elvirey gets the idea of using Granny's quilting pieces as chink, and when Pap arrives home safe and sound, he finally smiles when he sees their "log cabin quilt." He announces that "Mam would be proud," and the family is finally united and on the way to happiness. This thoughtful, expressive picture book deals with the westward expansion and points out the hardships and the thinking of that time. The "down home" dialogue makes a good read aloud.

Krisher, Trudy. **Spite Fences**. New York: Delacorte Press, 1994. 283p. $14.95. ISBN 0-385-32088-4, 0-440-22016-5pa.

Maggie Pugh's family is struggling financially, so when she's offered a job cleaning a man's house, she accepts it. She never sees the man she's working for but, by observing his reading material and the things he has lying around the house, begins to picture him. To her horror, she discovers he is a Black activist, working on changing life for the Blacks in her Georgia town in 1960. She is from a poor White family, but to be working for a Black man is unheard of. As she gets to know her employer, she begins to see life from a totally different perspective, questioning why Blacks have to use different bathrooms and drinking fountains and why they have a separate park. Her turmoil is heightened when she secretly witnesses her Black friend, Zeke, being beaten and left for dead by a band of White men seeking revenge for the activists being in town. This stunning, powerful novel is a must when studying the Civil Rights movement. It is an excellent choice to use along with Christopher Curtis's *The Watsons Go to Birmingham—1963*.

MacLachlan, Patricia. **Sarah, Plain and Tall**. This is the story of a family settling on the plains during the westward movement. *See* HIGH INTEREST—LOW READING LEVEL.

McCully, Emily Arnold. **The Ballot Box Battle**. The story of women's suffrage is told through this biography of Elizabeth Stanton. *See* BIOGRAPHIES.

————. **The Bobbin Girl**. New York: Dial Books for Young Readers, 1996. 34p. $16.00. ISBN 0-8037-1827-6 (trade), 0-8037-1828-4 (lib. bdg.).

> Lowell, Massachusetts, was established as a mill town in the 1820s with the mills controlling the town and everyone in it. Women were hired because their wages were lower, but even with substandard wages, they could still earn more at the mills than at other jobs. However, with increased production, the price for cotton cloth went down and so did the women's wages. In 1834, the first walkout was organized to protest the unfair working conditions. This picture book, loosely inspired by Harriet Hanson Robinson, who wrote about her experiences during this time, features 10-year-old Rebecca Putney, who works as a bobbin girl in the mills. Through her eyes, we see the toll the difficult conditions took on the women's lives, often endangering, maiming, and even killing them. Rebecca joins the women in the 1834 walkout. Though it did not change the mill owner's policies, it did empower women to continue the struggle and eventually make headway. This book is excellent to use along with Katherine Paterson's 1991 work, *Lyddie*, which deals with women in the textile mills in greater depth.

Miller, Brandon Marie. **Buffalo Gals: Women of the Old West**. Minneapolis, MN: Lerner, 1995. 88p. $15.00. ISBN 0-8225-1730-2.

> One of the best ways to learn about life during a particular time is from primary sources—actual writings, speeches, journal entries, photographs, and drawings from the time period. All these sources are used in this book to tell the story of the westward movement through the eyes of the brave and not so brave women who experienced this adventure. This book describes women's life on the wagon trail: cooking, camping, caring for the children, childbirth, illness, hunger, enemy attacks, and death; but it also relates the joys of breathtaking scenery, camaraderie, and of the woman's sense of accomplishment. Once they completed the trek, homes had to be set up and a new life begun. An abundance of black-and-white photographs augment the text to make this an excellent source for information on women's role in the development of the West.

Moeri, Louise. **Save Queen of Sheba**. New York: E. P. Dutton, 1981. 116p. $10.95. ISBN 0-525-33202-2, 0-14-037148-6pa.

The wagon train that King David and Queen of Sheba are on becomes disjointed and scattered, making them the perfect target for a Sioux attack. When the attack happens the wagons don't have time to get into a circle, allowing the Sioux to kill every adult. Only the two children miraculously survive. King David, the big brother, gathers a sack of cornmeal, a few apples, and a rifle and bullets and sets out to find the rest of the wagon train, hoping they have survived because they were farther ahead. Keeping his six-year-old sister, Queen of Sheba, satisfied and tuned in to survival is a challenge. Rather than appreciate that she's alive and that they have any food at all, she complains because the cornmeal is uncooked and she doesn't have the comforts of home. When the food supply is nearly gone and the situation is looking dismal and hopeless, Queen of Sheba wanders off, causing them to lose a day of travel and possibly their lives. However, once again David is ingenious and uses survival techniques to overcome injury, pain, hunger, thirst, and a bratty little sister, and he leads them to safety. The story is historically correct and accurately chronicles how it would have been to survive on the prairie at that time. Queen of Sheba thinks only of herself and lives in her make-believe world, and King David plays the part of the big brother, understanding that survival is up to him.

Nelson, Theresa. **And One for All**. New York: Orchard, 1989. 182p. $13.00. ISBN 0-531-05804-2 (trade), 0-531-08404-3 (lib. bdg.), 0-440-40456-8pa.

It has taken nearly 20 years before authors began to write fictional accounts about the Vietnam War, but we now have some excellent books on that subject, this one being one of the best. This moving story of a family in the 1960s, who struggle with the war is told by the 12-year-old sister, Geraldine. Mama is dead set against the war, and as the mother of a teenage son, she is frightened and worried that her son will be called to active duty. Daddy is a decorated World War II veteran and believes people must do their duty for their country. Wing, the teenage brother, has a difficult time in school, and Mama has struggled to help him. A few weeks before high-school graduation, after some problems, Wing signs up with the Marines. Mama's worst nightmare comes true. He is sent to Vietnam and never comes home. This moving and socially significant story is told in a simple, innocent manner through the eyes of the little sister who dearly loves her big brother, accurately depicting the feelings of this time.

O'Dell, Scott. **Sing Down the Moon**. Boston: Dell, 1970. 137p. $14.00. ISBN 0-395-10919-1, 0-440-97975-7pa.

As a 14-year-old, Bright Morning, a Navajo girl, is content to live the way her family has lived for centuries in the red buttes of the Canyon de Chelly in Arizona. She helps tend the sheep and the gardens, fields, and orchards and appreciates the natural beauty around her. All that changes dramatically when Spanish slavers capture Bright Morning and her friend Running Bird. They are taken to work as slaves for wealthy Spaniards until they manage to escape and return home. They are set-tled in, and life seems good again until 1864, when Long Knives—U.S. soldiers led by Kit Carson—order them to move from their lovely valley to Fort Sumner, New Mexico. All crops and livestock are burned, so the Navajos are forced to go on the deadly 300-mile walk, known as the Long Walk. It is unclear exactly how many Navajos died along the way, but 8,491 people reached the fort and were forced to remain there until 1868, while smallpox and other diseases killed more than 1,500 of them. Bright Morning and her family survive and after some time and hard-ship manage to get back to their beloved Canyon de Chelly. This book involves a spunky Navajo girl who has an important story to tell, but the main theme is her people's will to live and refusal to allow their culture to die. Vivid descriptions of Navajo life are given, including their food, clothing, mores, and ways of thinking.

————. **Streams to the River, River to the Sea: A Novel of Sacagawea**. Boston: Houghton Mifflin, 1986. 191p. $14.95. ISBN 0-395-40430-4.
When President Thomas Jefferson decides to have the Northwest explored—a wilderness no White man has ever seen—he chooses two U.S. Army officers to lead the exploration: Meriwether Lewis, age 29, and William Clark, 33. They meet up with Sacagawea, a Shoshone Indian, who acts as their interpreter and guide. O'Dell tells this story from Sacagawea's perspective, making it a powerful and realistic account. She has the monumental task of caring for her infant, dealing with an abusive husband, and getting the band of explorers to the Columbia River and finally to the Pacific Ocean. O'Dell used the actual journals of Lewis and Clark to gain information, making her saga historically accurate. Many tales abound about Captain Clark's affection for Sacagawea, who he called Janey, but the issue is handled tactfully and appropriately for young readers. Reading this account makes readers feel as if they are actually on the trip with the explorers, traveling 4,000 miles on a journey that still ranks as one of the most daring and courageous in the history of the United States. Extensive explanations are given about the flora and fauna and bodies of water in this pristine land, making it a good tie-in with science to study what the environment was like before the West was settled.

Panzer, Nora, ed. **Celebrate America: In Poetry and Art**. Famous art pieces and American poetry tell America's story. *See* FINE ARTS.

Parker, Nancy Winslow. **Locks, Crocs, & Skeeters: The Story of the Panama Canal**. The building of the Panama Canal is told through poetry and biographies. *See* UNIQUE PRESENTATIONS.

Paterson, Katherine. **Jip: His Story**. Jip, an orphan, becomes involved with the movement to free the slaves after his true identify is revealed. *See* GREATEST OF THE LATEST.

————. **Lyddie**. New York: Lodestar Books, 1991. 182p. $14.95. ISBN 0-525-67338-5.

> Lyddie and her brother are forced to work for neighbors in payment of the debts their mother owed when she took the babies and fled their Vermont farm in 1843. Lyddie despises her work in the tavern, but it is there she hears about work for young women in Lowell, Massachusetts, in the textile mills. She runs away to Lowell and begins life as a factory girl. Lyddie tells about the long hours and the dangerous, disease-threatening working conditions in the textile mills at that time. She becomes friends with Diana, who is organizing a demand for better working conditions, but this is dangerous and may cause her to lose her job. This is an important time in U.S. history for women and all workers, and Lyddie and her coworkers helped to pave the way for modern industry. For other sources on this topic, see *The Bobbin Girl*, by Emily Arnold McCully, and Avi's *Beyond the Western Sea: Book Two, Lord Kirkle's Money*, reviewed in this chapter.

Paulsen, Gary. **Nightjohn**. New York: Delacorte Press, 1993. 92p. $14.00. ISBN 0-385-30838-8.

> Sarny, a 12-year-old Black slave on the Waller plantation, tells this short, poignant, historically accurate story of Nightjohn, a slave who escaped to freedom in the North but who is committed to going back to help his fellowmen. In her own dialect, Sarny tells about the harsh life as a slave and the great lengths the slave owners go to keep the slaves from being educated about anything other than their own plantation environment. They are deliberately kept from learning to read or write or do any kind of math, because information is a powerful tool and could possibly work against the owners. Sarny first sees Nightjohn when he has been stripped of his clothes and is being whipped and sent out to the fields to work. At night he offers to trade some of her saved tobacco for learning letters and numbers, which he draws in the dirt. Sarny is fascinated by these squiggles and learns quickly. However, Waller catches her, beats her, shackles Mammy, and brutally leaves her hanging until one of them will tell who's teaching Sarny to read. Nightjohn admits he's the teacher, and as punishment a toe is cut off of each foot. He successfully runs away again but returns once again to teach "pit school" to slaves at night, using a catalog as a textbook. This powerful novel is a "must" when studying slavery and plantation life in America. A sequel, *Sarny*, has recently been published.

Polacco, Patricia. **Pink and Say**. New York: Philomel Books, 1994. 48p. $15.95. ISBN 0-399-22671-0.

> Patricia Polacco has the marvelous ability to take a family story and share it through poignant and moving picture books. This is the

story of a White boy from Ohio, Sheldon Russell Curtis—better known as Say—who was Polacco's great-great-grandfather. Say, a flag carrier for the Union Army, runs away and is shot as he is deserting. He is found by a Black boy, Pinkus Aylee—better known as Pink—who has become separated from his northern regiment. Pink takes Say home to his mother, Moe Moe Bay, who nurses them both back to health. Moe Moe is the only person left on a big Southern estate where she has been a slave until the war drove her master away. When they have recovered, Say wants to return home to Ohio, but Pink insists they go back to fight. They are captured by the South and sent to Andersonville Prison, where Pink is hanged almost immediately, but Say lives to tell their story. This powerful book fits well with Gary Paulsen's *Nightjohn*, and James Lincoln and Christopher Collier's *With Every Drop of Blood*.

Rostkowski, Margaret I. **After the Dancing Days**. New York: Harper & Row, 1986. 217p. $13.89. ISBN 0-06-025077-1 (trade), 0-06-025078-X (lib. bdg.), 0-06-440248-7pa.

Americans are often chided for not welcoming the Vietnam veterans when they returned from war in the same way that we celebrated the return of veterans from other wars, but this novel points out how there were those from other wars who weren't celebrated—especially if they weren't whole and pleasant to look at. Annie's father, a prominent doctor in Kansas City, does a tour of duty as a military doctor during World War I. Once home, he chooses to work with the disfigured, burned, and shunned young men at the veteran's hospital rather than return to his prestigious position at the local private hospital. Annie's mother is appalled, but Annie becomes interested and goes to the hospital to meet some of her father's patients. She discovers that these disabled young men are lonely and forgotten and face a dismal future, but they are warm and friendly and eager to be friends. She learns a great deal about the war and also gains a new appreciation for those less fortunate than she, even when it brings disdain from her family and friends. The character development is excellent as we watch Annie grow from a spoiled rich kid to an understanding, caring young woman.

Ruby, Lois. **Steal Away Home**. The story of the Underground Railroad and freedom for slaves is told in this time-travel book. *See* UNIQUE PRESENTATIONS.

San Souci, Robert. **The Red Heels**. A traveling shoemaker falls in love with one of his customers who has magic red shoes that allow them to dance to the moon. This fanciful story gives a good idea about what life was like in New England in colonial times. *See* MYTHS, FOLKTALES, AND LEGENDS.

———. **Sootface: An Ojibwa Cinderella Story**. Illus. Daniel San Souci. In this Native American version of "Cinderella" Sootface is the only woman who can see what the young brave has in his hands, making her his choice for a wife. *See* MYTHS, FOLKTALES, AND LEGENDS.

Schroeder, Alan. **Minty: A Story of Young Harriet Tubman**. Illus. Jerry Pinkney. This biography of Harriet Tubman's childhood gives excellent background into her early life which strongly affected her later work with the Underground Railroad. *See* BIOGRAPHIES.

Snyder, Zilpha Keatley. **Cat Running**. New York: Delacorte Press, 1994. 168p. $14.95. ISBN 0-385-31056-0.
> When the Great Depression hits, Catherine, better known as Cat, is affected little because her father owns a hardware store, and business continues as usual for quite some time. Cat is the fastest runner in the school and has hopes of winning the Winner's Grand Finale until a new boy, Zane Perkins, enrolls. She is angry with him because he might possibly beat her, yet she's curious about him because he eats strange things and dresses very shabbily, wearing the same ill-fitting clothing every day. Cat feels sorry for herself because her father is domineering and refuses to allow her to wear slacks for the race, even though her teacher encourages it. One day while on a practice run, Cat ends up outside town where a shantytown made up of Dustbowl refugees has sprung up. She discovers that Zane and his family live there in utter poverty, and as she becomes involved with the family she learns that the strife in her home is trivial compared to the hunger and illness experienced in Zane's family. For the first time in her life Cat is confronted with the horrors of poverty, prejudice, and life-threatening illness. She is able to set her own problems aside and learns to help those in need, even when it jeopardizes her own well-being. The character of Cat is well developed as she goes on a journey of self-discovery and matures. A clear picture of life during the Great Depression is described as seen from a young teenager's eyes.

Speare, Elizabeth George. **The Sign of the Beaver**. A young boy in the 1700s learns to depend on the wisdom and experience of a Native American boy to survive in the wilderness of Maine. *See* SCIENCE.

————. **The Witch of Blackbird Pond**. Kit Tyler arrives in Connecticut from Barbados in 1687. She finds herself in the Puritan world and after a series of events is declared a witch. This is a superb representation of Puritan life. *See* ENGLISH—CLASSICS.

Taylor, Mildred D. **Roll of Thunder, Hear My Cry**. New York: The Dial Press, 1976. 276p. $15.00. ISBN 0-8037-7473-7.
> Set in Mississippi during the Great Depression, this is the story of the Logans, a feisty Black family who seek a good life. Life is difficult for them, but they own their own farm, and the mother is a teacher at the local Black school. They are fiercely proud of their farm and will do anything

to protect it. Mildred Taylor carefully weaves a story showing the difficulties experienced by Black people at that time and points out the inequities heaped upon them and how they handle them in a subtle, positive way. The story is told through the eyes of Cassie Logan, the oldest child, who insists on fairness and justice from everyone, including her own family, and she will go to any length to see that justice prevails. The love within the family, their own fighting spirit, and their can-do attitude make the Logan family one you'll never forget. The book has a powerful message as well as being historically accurate, which earned it the Newbery Award in 1977. The sequel, *Let the Circle Be Unbroken*, continues beyond the depression and follows the various family members as they grow up.

Turner, Ann. **Grass Songs**. Illus. Barry Moser. When a husband decided to pick up stakes and move westward, the pioneer women had no choice but to go along. This book of poetry expresses the feelings of women, most hating it but some feeling freed by and delighted with the move. *See* POETRY.

———. **Mississippi Mud: Three Prairie Journals**. Illus. Robert J. Blake. The children of a family traveling west in a wagon train record their experiences through poetry. *See* POETRY.

Van Zandt, Eleanor. **A History of the United States Through Art**. The story of the United States is told using famous works of art. *See* FINE ARTS.

Wisniewski, David. **The Wave of the Sea-Wolf**. New York: Clarion Books, 1994. 32p. $16.95. ISBN 0-395-66478-0.
Folklore of the Native American tribes in the Pacific Northwest is presented in this tale that attempts to explain the unusual waves that occasionally hit the mouth of the bay, now known as Lituya Bay. In actuality, there is an earthquake fault under the bay causing the unusual disturbance, but the Native Americans didn't know that so they explained it by using the legend of Gonakadet, also known as the Sea-Wolf. This spirit is also the bearer of wealth and good fortune, but when the exceptionally large waves hit, the people attribute this to the Sea-Wolf. The young princess, Kchokeen, goes to pick berries near the bay. Her parents warn her to stay away from the mouth of the bay because of the dangerous waves, but she disobeys, goes too close to the mouth, and is hit by a huge wave, which causes her to fall into the water. Luckily she falls into the trunk of a huge tree. While her friends run to get help, she is befriended by a bear, and after being rescued she is given the ability to predict when Gonakadet is traveling to the bay and is able to warn the fishermen. The cut-paper pictures vividly describe Native American life, and information at the end of the book tells more about the tribes.

Yep, Laurence. **Dragon's Gate**. New York: HarperCollins, 1993. 273p. $15.00. ISBN 0-06-022971-3 (trade), 0-06-022972-1 (lib. bdg.).

The building of the transcontinental railroad was an amazing feat, but chiseling the path through the Sierra Nevada in California was the most difficult part of the construction. The human toll is seldom discussed, but Laurence Yep uses a family of Chinese immigrants to tell the story of the construction. The Chinese workers left China for America with hopes of becoming wealthy and important and then returning to China with new status. Many of them flocked to the railroad because it was the only work they could get, but they were essentially slaves, forced to work long hours with little food, under brutally dangerous working conditions, bitter cold, poor pay, and discrimination. The story of the Chinese workers' part in the building of the railroad is told through a young man, Otter, who secretly leaves China and joins his father and uncle in America, only to find that they hadn't been telling the truth in their letters, which had given glowing descriptions of their new lives. Otter goes to work on the railroad and quickly learns about the harshness of life and how little regard the railroad bosses have for the Chinese and other immigrants. Many lives were lost on the job because of these dreadful living conditions. Excellent descriptions are given of the drilling, blasting, and hauling of the rock. A meager attempt at striking over the working conditions is made, but it only made matters worse. This is an important novel to use when studying westward expansion and California history.

Chapter 14

SOCIAL STUDIES—ANCIENT AND EARLY CULTURES

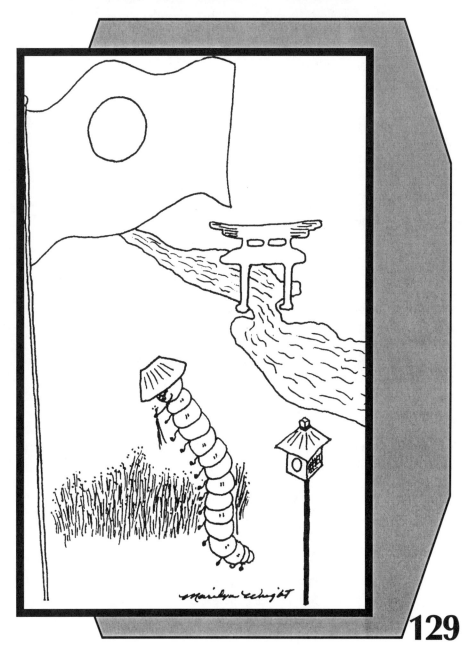

This section covers a broad range of topics both geographically and historically. Particular emphasis is placed on the cultures of early man, ancient China, India, Japan, Europe, the Middle East, Greece, Rome, and Egypt as well as the Middle Ages, the Renaissance, and Latin American cultures. Many myths, legends, and folktales have been included because they tell a great deal about life in past cultures and because so many outstanding works concentrating on ancient and early cultures are now available.

Bahous, Sally. **Sitti and the Cats**. This Persian tale tells the story of the town's wise old woman and includes Persian writing and special pieces of information about that culture. *See* MYTHS, FOLKTALES, AND LEGENDS.

Bateson-Hill, Margaret. **Lao Lao of Dragon Mountain**. Chinese text Manyee Wan, illus. Francesca Pelizzoli, paper cuts Sha-Liu Qu. An Ancient Chinese tale is told using paper cuts. The Chinese translation and directions for paper cuts are included. *See* FINE ARTS.

Beshore, George. **Science in Ancient China**. Included in this work are the history and the scientific developments of ancient China. *See* SCIENCE.

——. **Science in Early Islamic Culture**. This work traces the scientific and mathematic advancements made during the Islamic empire. *See* SCIENCE.

Birch, David. **The King's Chessboard**. Illus. Devis Grebu. Set in ancient India, this is a retelling of the ancient story of rice that is doubled in amount every day and of something that starts out simply yet ends up to be enormous sums. *See* MATHEMATICS.

Camille, Eric A. **The Three Princes: A Tale from the Middle East**. In this Middle Eastern tale a princess decides which man to choose for her husband. *See* MYTHS, FOLKTALES, AND LEGENDS.

Climo, Shirley. **Atalanta's Race: A Greek Myth**. This is a retelling of the Greek myth. *See* MYTHS, FOLKTALES, AND LEGENDS.

Cowley, Marjorie. **Dar and the Spear-Thrower**. New York: Clarion Books, 1994. 118p. $13.95. ISBN 0-395-68132-4.
> Life was difficult during the Ice Age, and only the most hearty survived. Clans were small because of the difficulty of feeding and caring for large numbers of people. Dar, a small 13-year-old knows he is expected to become the next leader of the clan, but he doubts his abilities. His uncle is becoming impatient with his lack of leadership, and through Dar's story the reader learns what life was like for early man. Good explanations about food, clothing, and living conditions are given as well as the social structure of the community.

Cushman, Karen. **Catherine, Called Birdy**. Life in medieval England in 1290 is well described by Catherine, a spunky 14-year-old who refuses to marry Shaggy Beard, the man her father says she must marry. The story is told with diary entries. *See* UNIQUE PRESENTATIONS.

————. **The Midwife's Apprentice**. New York: Clarion Books, 1995. 122p. $10.95. ISBN 0-395-69229-6, 0-06440630-Xpa.
> A homeless girl, known only as Brat, is found in a dung heap by the local midwife, who renames her Beetle and gives her food and a place to sleep in return for work. Set in fourteenth-century England, the midwife is the local healer as well as the person who helps bring babies into the world. Life during this time is described as Beetle learns midwifery and healing from Jane Sharp, the person who took her in. Beetle learns what each herb will do and how to use the bounty in the forest and along the hillsides to prepare food as well as medicines. As she gains knowledge and self-confidence, Beetle also demands a real name, Alyce. Alyce continues to advance and learn from Jane as well as the world around her. This brief work gives a great deal of information about the Middle Ages, particularly about medicine and healing at that time.

Delacre, Lulu. **Golden Tales: Myths, Legends, and Folktales from Latin America**. This is a collection of Latin American folktales. *See* MYTHS, FOLKTALES, AND LEGENDS.

Demi. **The Dragon's Tale and Other Animal Fables of the Chinese Zodiac**. A Chinese tale and description of the zodiac are presented in this colorful and descriptive work. *See* MYTHS, FOLKTALES, AND LEGENDS.

————. **The Magic Tapestry**. Ancient China is vividly illustrated in this work of art. *See* MYTHS, FOLKTALES, AND LEGENDS.

―――. **One Grain of Rice: A Mathematical Folktale**. This Indian folktale tells the ancient story of a master rewarding a faithful servant with one grain of rice that doubles every day, accumulating vast amounts of rice. *See* MATHEMATICS.

Denzel, Justin. **Boy of the Painted Cave**. New York: Philomel Books, 1988. 158p. $14.95. ISBN 0-399-21559-X, 0-698-11377-2pa.

> The study of early man is brought alive through Tao, a 14-year-old crippled boy who is banished from his tribe because he is not useful to it and cannot contribute as well as the others. What he really wants to do is paint and draw on the walls of caves, but only the Chosen One is allowed to do this. After his banishment Tao is befriended by a wolf dog and an old shaman, Graybeard, who is traveling through and helps him to sort out his life. Reading about Tao's life and his struggle for survival is an exciting way to learn about life 18,000 years ago. Cave paintings, the chronicles of that time, are well described. This book is now available in paperback, making it an excellent source to use as a core literature book when studying early man.

Dickinson, Peter. **A Bone from a Dry Sea**. New York: Delacorte Press, 1992. 199p. $16.00. ISBN 0-385-30821-3.

> Two stories, 4 million years apart, are told in alternating chapters. An intelligent female child, Li, tells the story of a prehistoric group who live in and around the sea, totally dependent on the water for survival. They have no real spoken language but use calls to signify their needs and what they mean. The child realizes she is different from the others, qualifying her to tell the story of her group. The present-day child, Vinny, also an intelligent female, goes on a dig with her father, a famous archaeologist, and experiences the harsh and difficult life in the wilds. While digging, she discovers how boring and tedious the work is, and she learns about the fierce competition and backbiting among the archaeologists. Both civilizations are followed in alternating chapters until members of the present-day group discover some remains of the early civilization. Many theories are made by the archaeological group in an attempt to decode what the early culture was. It's fun to compare these theories with the information given by Li.

Furlong, Monica. **Juniper**. Set in early medieval times, Juniper, the herbalist and healer, describes how she became magical with the help of her godmother, Euny. This is a prequel to *Wise Child*. *See* ENGLISH—CLASSICS.

―――. **Wise Child**. Abandoned by her parents, Wise Child is assigned to live with Juniper, who loves her and trains her to use herbs and magic. During medieval times herbalists were turned to in time of illness, but the church saw them as a threat to its power and regarded them as witches. This portrayal of life at that time has a good dose of magic thrown in. *See* ENGLISH—CLASSICS.

Gay, Kathlyn. **Science in Ancient Greece**. The information in this book describes scientific advancements in ancient Greece and how they related to the people's culture. *See* SCIENCE.

Gravett, Christopher. **The Knight's Handbook: How to Become a Champion in Shining Armor**. This how-to book on the Middle Ages gives patterns for making things used by knights. *See* FINE ARTS.

Hastings, Selina. **Sir Gawain and the Loathly Lady**. This is a classic story about King Arthur and his knights. *See* MYTHS, FOLKTALES, AND LEGENDS.

Ho, Minfong. **Maples in the Mist: Children's Poems from the Tang Dynasty**. This outstanding collection of poems about ancient China includes Chinese characters and beautiful artwork. *See* POETRY.

Kurtz, Jane. **Miro in the Kingdom of the Sun**. This tale, set during the Inca empire, is about a girl who is looking for the water that will save the Inca prince. *See* MYTHS, FOLKTALES, AND LEGENDS.

Langley, Andrew, and Philip De Souza. **The Roman News**. A newspaper format is used to describe Roman civilization. *See* UNIQUE PRESENTATIONS.

Lasky, Kathryn. **The Librarian Who Measured the Earth**. The biography of Eratosthenes, the ancient Greek mathematician, scientist, author and geographer, is told in a delightful, informative manner. *See* MATHEMATICS.

Lewin, Ted. **Sacred River**. New York: Clarion Books, 1994. 35p. $14.95. ISBN 0-395-69846-4.
>   The Ganges River, the sacred river of India, flows through the ancient city of Benares. The highest goal in the life of Hindus is to make a pilgrimage to Benares and purify their souls by bathing in the Ganges. Ted Lewin and his wife traveled to Benares and were fascinated by the myriad of people who made the pilgrimage and were cleansed and purified. The story begins in the early morning and follows the activities of the people as the day proceeds. The text is minimal, but the full-page paintings beautifully portray the city, the river, the transportation, the people, customs and rituals, and the activities included in this purification. This is an outstanding source to use when studying ancient India or the Hindu religion.

Lobel, Anita. **The Dwarf Giant**. A kingdom in ancient Japan is saved from an evil dwarf's takeover. Excellent examples of Japanese art are included. *See* FINE ARTS.

London, Jonathan. **Ali, Child of the Desert**. Illus. Ted Lewin. New York: Lothrop, Lee & Shepard, 1997. Unpaged. $16.00. ISBN 0-688-12560-3 (trade), 0-688-12561-1 (lib. bdg.).

Ali is finally old enough to travel with his father to the Moroccan market at the edge of the Sahara Desert on his faithful camel, Jabad, but a sandstorm arises, and he is separated from his father and the camel herd. He is rescued by a herdsman and is reunited with his father. The story is a simple one, and the boy is young, but the descriptions of Arab life—the foods eaten, the dependency on the animals, the clothing, the housing, the nomadic life, and the people's means of survival—are beautifully described, making it the perfect tie-in to study of the Arab world. The large, brightly colored illustrations are worth the price of the book.

Lorenz, Albert, with Joy Schleh. **Metropolis: Ten Cities, Ten Centuries**. New York: Harry N. Abrams, 1996. 64p. $20.00. ISBN 0-8109-4284-4.

This unique and intriguing book explores ten major cities around the world at their time of major importance. Each is described and explained through a variety of methods covering six oversize pages. The first and second pages for each city show intricate drawings, with enlarged maps that show how the city fits into the world around it, along with written information about the city and a list of the important events occurring in that city during the century. The third and fourth pages narrow down to the city itself, including what seems like every nook and cranny of the city. Albert Lorenz, an architect, uses his knowledge and skills to give the reader a visual feast using fine line drawings to give intricate details. Small boxes around the edges of each page give a timetable and a drawing to show important happenings around the world during the century presented. Pages five and six of each city use text and drawings to depict everyday life in the city at that time. Lorenz presents Jerusalem in the eleventh century, Paris in the twelfth century, a Mongol tent city in the thirteenth century, Koblenz during the fourteenth century to describe how the Black Plague spread, Lisbon in the fifteenth century to present the Age of Discovery, Florence during the sixteenth century to depict the Renaissance, Osaka in the seventeenth century, Vienna in the eighteenth century, London in the nineteenth century, and, finally, New York in the twentieth century to represent modern cities. This fascinating book is jammed with information that teaches about history, culture, and the arts.

Louie, Ai-Ling. **Yeh-Shen: A Cinderella Story from China**. This is an ancient Chinese version of "Cinderella," surprisingly similar to our modern-day telling. *See* MYTHS, FOLKTALES, AND LEGENDS.

Mann, Kenny. **Ghana, Mali, Songhay: The Western Sudan**. Parsippany, NJ: Dillon Press, 1996. 108p. (African Kingdoms of the Past, Book 1). $16.00. ISBN 0-87518-656-4, 0-382-39176-3pa.

Finding good information on ancient Africa is always a challenge, but the African Kingdoms of the Past series has helped to solve that problem. This volume on the Western Sudan gives excellent, detailed information through text, colorful illustrations, maps, drawings, sketches and photographs, and a time line. The ancient history of the areas is traced in detail, but it is also tied in with what is happening in those parts of the world today. This is a marvelous resource to use when teaching old Africa.

Mayo, Margaret. **Mythical Birds and Beasts from Many Lands**. Illus. Jane Ray. In this volume ten myths from around the world involve mythical animals. *See* MYTHS, FOLKTALES, AND LEGENDS.

McMullan, Kate. **Under the Mummy's Spell**. New York: Farrar, Straus & Giroux, 1992. 214p. $16.00. ISBN 0-374-38033-3.

Two stories are told at the same time: One is set in modern times and involves Peter Harring, a child ignored by his mother and often left on his own; the other tells of Nephia, the daughter of the Pharaoh Amenhut in Egypt in the year XVI. Peter meets Nephia in the Metropolitan Museum of Art where she is a mummy in an Egyptian display. His buddy, Rodent, dares him to kiss the mummy's picture painted on the coffin, and as he does, Peter is suddenly under the spell of Nephia, the princess. She involves him in the mystery of her death, and high adventure takes place. Peter's story is told in regular print, and in alternating chapters Nephia's story is written in italics. Nephia's story reveals a great deal of information about ancient Egypt, and it makes an excellent read aloud when studying ancient Egypt.

Mellinkoff, Pamela. **Plots and Players**. New York: Bedrick/Blackie, 1988. 160p. $9.95. ISBN 0-87226-406-8.

Set in Shakespeare's time, this multifaceted work involves three children—Robin, Philip, and Frances Fernandez. Their parents want a good life for the children, but Robin becomes involved with William Shakespeare, an offbeat character who wants to create plays. He wants Robin to be in these plays, which is frightening to Robin's parents because they are exiled Jews from Portugal and can't afford to have attention drawn to them. This is the main premise of the story, but many other subplots enter in, including one about saving the life of Queen Elizabeth's Jewish doctor who has been falsely accused of spying for Spain. Adventure and mystery abound along with an accurate picture of what life was like in London during Shakespeare's time. The reader needs some background knowledge to understand some of the happenings, making this an excellent source to use when studying this time period.

Moss, Carol. **Science in Ancient Mesopotamia**. The information in this book describes the scientific developments in Mesopotamia. *See* SCIENCE.

Müller, Claudia. **The Timeline of World Costume: From Fig Leaf to Street Fashion**. This unusual work illustrates types of clothing and costumes worn in societies around the world from 3000 B.C. through the twentieth century. The book is not bound, but the pages fold onto one another, allowing the user to stretch the pages out into one huge timeline. If students need information on clothing from a particular geographical area at a particular time, this book will have it. *See* UNIQUE PRESENTATIONS.

Patent, Dorothy Hinshaw. **Quetzal, Sacred Bird of the Cloud Forest**. New York: Morrow Junior Books, 1996. 40p. $16.00. ISBN 0-688-12662-6 (trade), 0-688-12663-4 (lib. bdg.).
> The history of the Aztecs and the Mayans of Central America is told through the quetzal, the national bird of Guatemala. The bird has great symbolic meaning to the present-day people and played a big role in the early civilizations. All aspects of the cultures, the history, the land and the people—past and present—have been influenced by the quetzal. Several sections deal with the bird itself—how it lives, mates, eats, raises its chicks, and adjusts to the present environment. The muted paintings show the landscape, historical aspects, and the beauty of the bird. This is an interesting approach to tie the past and the present together.

Peterson, Gail. **Greg Hildebrandt's Book of Three-Dimensional Dragons**. Five large, colorful dragons—including the wyvern dragon, the Amphiptere, the Lindworm, a Chinese dragon, and the Dragon of St. George—all pop up when this book is opened. The text explains each legendary dragon as it appears in history and literature. *See* UNIQUE PRESENTATIONS.

Powell, Anton, and Philip Steele. **The Greek News**. Ancient Greek civilization is presented in a newspaper format. *See* UNIQUE PRESENTATIONS.

Reddix, Valerie. **Dragon Kite of the Autumn Moon**. Illus. Jean Tseng and Mou-sien Tseng. New York: Lothrop, Lee & Shepard, 1991. $14.00. ISBN 0-688-11030-4 (trade), 0-688-11031-2 (lib. bdg.).
> The ancient Chinese custom of a special Kite's Day in the ninth month of the year, six days before the rising of the full moon, originated in China before the seventh century. Tradition says that the kites must be set free at the end of the day and burned when they fall to the Earth,

thereby taking misfortune with them. Tad-Tin's grandfather always makes a new kite for Kite's Day, but this year grandfather is ill and is unable to make a kite. The only kite Tad-Tin has is a huge, beautiful dragon kite that Grandfather made for him when he was born. He doesn't want to fly and burn that kite, but he finally gets up the courage to fly the beautiful dragon, which pleases Grandfather. This is a good source to use when studying ancient China or when studying or making kites. The paintings of the dragon kite and the descriptions of it are excellent.

Singer, Isaac Bashevis. **The Topsy-Turvy Emperor of China**. Trans. Elizabeth Shub, illus. Julian Jusim. New York: Farrar, Straus & Giroux, 1996. 32p. $16.00. ISBN 0-374-37681-6.

The good emperor of China dies, leaving behind his mean and ugly son, Cho Cho Shang. Because he is repulsive, nasty, and evil, he wants everyone else to be the same way. As emperor, he declares that everything is exactly the opposite of the way it used to be. Anything beautiful is replaced with everything ugly, coarse, hideous, and unjust, and all the beautiful artwork is destroyed and replaced with smudges and smears. He even marries an ugly, atrocious woman. Flowers and growing things are uprooted, women are forced to discard their beautiful robes and dress in ill-cut, glaring-colored rags with dyed hair, their eyebrows plucked out, their nails painted black, and they have to have tiny, bound, disabled feet. The men shave half their beards, and everything joyful is forbidden. Only bad things are allowed. Anyone who doesn't comply is tortured and hanged. One man, Chung Mi Pu, is not fooled by the emperor. He is in charge of the royal museum of the emperor's palace, and on the outside he appears to go along with all the absurdity, but he is secretly hiding many of the old royal paintings and treasures. He is also hiding his beautiful daughter, Min Lu. The emperor and the empress have a son, Ling Ling, who is handsome and intelligent and becomes convinced early on in his life that things are mixed up. His life is miserable until Chung Mi Pu introduces him to Min Lu. Eventually good triumphs over evil, and the people rebel, thanks to Ling Ling. The evil emperor is killed, and the empress dies from laughter. Ling Ling and Min Lu are married and go on to rule with truth, goodness, and beauty. This delightful story gives the reader a great deal of information about ancient China through the text and the illustrations. The pages are made to look aged, which adds to the charm, and Chinese writing is included in many of the illustrations, making the book of even greater interest.

Snyder, Zilpha Keatley. **The Egypt Game**. Illus. Alton Raible. A group of friends invent an elaborate game about ancient Egypt based on facts learned at the local library. *See* ENGLISH—CLASSICS.

———. **Song of the Gargoyle**. New York: Delacorte Press, 1991. 232p. $15.00. ISBN 0-385-303017, 0-440-40898-9pa.

Tymmon, the son of the court jester, Komus, must flee the only home he's ever known because Komus has been abducted, and the kidnappers are looking for Tymmon. He doesn't know where to go, but he heads toward the forest, hoping for protection while on his quest to find his father. He is met by a huge beast who befriends him and seems to understand everything he says. Tymmon is not sure whether the beast is a huge dog or a gargoyle, a magical beast, but he prefers to see Troff as a gargoyle, hoping for protection and a bit of magic. It is never revealed what Troff really is—that is left up to the reader's imagination. Set during the Middle Ages, the two have many frightening and exciting adventures and end up at a castle that is under siege. After a series of exciting events, Tymmon is reunited with his father, and they are able to go back to their old castle because the evil baronet has been driven out, replaced by people who love Komus and Tymmon. A great deal of information about the Middle Ages is included along with the accounts of the adventures, making this an excellent core literature book or read aloud to use when studying this time period.

Sola, Michele. **Angela Weaves a Dream: The Story of a Young Maya Artist**. Photo. Jeffrey Jay Foxx. The importance and history of weaving in a Mayan village is described and photographed. *See* FINE ARTS.

Spivak, Dawnine. **Grass Sandals: The Travels of Basho**. Illus. Demi. The biography of Basho, an important writer and philosopher in seventeenth-century Japan, gives good insight into life at that time. *See* POETRY.

Stanley, Diane. **Fortune**. This Middle Eastern tale has outstanding artwork that shows life in this part of the world. *See* MYTHS, FOLKTALES, AND LEGENDS.

Stanley, Diane, and Peter Vennema. **Good Queen Bess: The Story of Elizabeth I of England**. This picture book with extended text gives an excellent biography of Elizabeth I. *See* BIOGRAPHY.

Staples, Suzanne Fisher. **Shabanu, Daughter of the Wind**. New York: Alfred A. Knopf, 1989. 240p. $20.00. ISBN 0-394-84815-2 (trade), 0-394-94815-7 (lib. bdg.), 0-679-81030-7pa.
　　　　This work is set in present-day Pakistan in the Cholistan Desert, but it aptly portrays life as it has been for centuries. Shabanu is excited because her sister, Phulan, will soon be married and the next year Shabanu, age 12, will marry the brother of Phulan's husband—both marriages arranged by her father. Shabanu is happy with her nomadic way of life taking care of the camels—her family's main source of income—but once a girl in this society becomes a woman, she must marry according to her father's wishes. The arrangement is fine with the sisters until the oldest brother is killed and Phulan must marry the younger brother, Shabanu's intended. Shabanu is then promised to a wealthy but despised

landowner, someone she finds distasteful and disgusting. By following Shabanu's family through the desert looking for food and water for the camels, much is learned about the Islamic culture and the nomadic way of life, which has changed little over time. The sequel, *Haveli*, follows Shabanu's life after she is married and has a daughter.

Stolz, Mary. **Bartholomew Fair**. New York: Greenwillow, 1990. 152p. $12.95. ISBN 0-688-09522-4, 0-688-11501-2pa.
During the Middle Ages, the local fair was a major event in people's lives. This book follows six people on the day of London's Bartholomew Fair, including Queen Elizabeth, a wealthy cloth merchant, a scullery maid, two schoolboys and an apprentice. Each person's actions are described as he or she prepares for the fair, travels to the fair, attends the fair, and ends the day after the fair is over. Each person, depending on his or her social status, sees the fair from a different perspective and experiences different aspects of the event. The activities of the day are described well and portray a picture of life at this time.

Tahan, Malba. **The Man Who Counted: A Collection of Mathematical Adventures**. A wise man travels throughout the Middle East and solves math problems. *See* MATHEMATICS.

Talbott, Hudson, and Mark Greenberg. **Amazon Diary: The Jungle Adventures of Alex Winters**. A tale of adventure is set in the present-day Amazon jungle. *See* UNIQUE PRESENTATIONS.

Tan, Amy. **The Moon Lady**. Illus. Gretchen Schields. New York: Macmillan, 1992. 32p. $16.95. ISBN 0-02-788830-4.
Amy Tan adapted this story from a chapter in her adult book *The Joy Luck Club* to tell the rituals of an old Chinese holiday, the Moon Festival. It begins in San Francisco with three grandchildren looking out Grandmother's window, making wishes. This reminds Grandmother of one of her earliest memories in China, the Moon Festival, at which time a secret wish could be made to the Moon Lady. On the day of the festival Ying-ying awakens early, eager to start the festivities, but the adults are in no hurry. She dresses in her new clothes but has trouble keeping them clean because of her restlessness. The family takes a boat out onto the local lake and have a big picnic, and the adults chat over tea and take naps. Ying-ying explores everything on the boat, going where she shouldn't, and gets in the way of a cook preparing eels. Her new clothes become filled with the eel's blood, and she knows she's in trouble. She falls off the boat and is picked up by a fisherman and his wife. They attempt to locate Ying-ying's boat, but can't find it, so they leave her on the shore, where she watches a play portraying the Moon Lady. She tries to make a wish to the Moon Lady and follows her backstage—only to discover it is a man playing the part and he isn't granting wishes. She then discovers the real moon is overhead, so she makes a wish to be found.

The wish comes true. Grandmother ends the story by discussing the idea of wishes with her granddaughters and which types of wishes are the best. This is a lovely story that gives the flavor of old China as seen through the eyes of a little girl.

Tanaka, Shelley. **Discovering the Iceman**. Illus. Laurie McGaw. New York: Hyperion/Madison Press, 1997. 48p. (I Was There). $16.95. ISBN 0-7868-0284-7.
   The accidental discovery of Iceman in 1991 added to our knowledge of how early man lived 4,000 years ago. In this book, beautiful color photographs show the area where the discovery was made and the actual remains and artifacts, and sketches and drawings depict the tools and weapons, clothing, food, homes, medicines, and cures of the day. Part One tells about the discovery and the people involved with the removal of the remains and artifacts. Part Two creates a fictional story to describe Iceman's life, and Part Three pulls together information from the past, tells how the information was gathered, and gives its relevance to us in the present day. A detailed time line telling what was happening around the world at the time of Iceman is included as well as a glossary, an index, and a bibliography of recommended readings.

Temple, Frances. **Beduins' Gazelle**. New York: Orchard, 1996. 150p. $15.95. ISBN 0-531-08869-3.
   This brief work vividly depicts nomadic Islamic life in the Middle East in 1302 and includes a love story between two young people. It is similar to *Shabanu*, (Suzanne Staples 1989), but is not as lengthy or as involved. Frances Temple had intended to write three works depicting the Middle Ages in Europe and Africa, but unfortunately she died the day this second book was completed. *Beduins' Gazelle* is a perfect tie-in for study of the Middle Ages.

Williams, Laura E. **The Long Silk Strand: A Grandmother's Legacy to Her Granddaughter**. Illus. Grayce Bochak. Honesdale, PA: Boyds Mills Press, 1995. 34p. $15.95. ISBN 1-56397-236-0.
   One evening long ago in ancient Japan, Grandmother began tying silk threads together, each one symbolizing an event in her life. As she tied, she told the life stories to her granddaughter, Yasuyo. After the 100th day the ball was as big as a bamboo basket, and there was no more thread to be tied. Grandmother died that night, taking the ball with her into the sky but leaving the very end hanging down in the garden. Yasuyo climbs the thread and reaches Grandmother high in the clouds. Grandmother invites her to stay forever with her, but when Yasuyo looks down and sees her loving father and mother, she decides to go back home, taking with her one special strand of silk with which to remember Grandmother. This is a wonderful story that shows Japanese customs, food, clothing, and culture. The subtle cut-paper illustrations give the story a mystical feeling.

Williams, Marcia. **The Iliad and the Odyssey**. A comic-book telling of *The Iliad* and *The Odyssey*. *See* UNIQUE PRESENTATIONS.

Wilson, Elizabeth B. **Bibles and Bestiaries: A Guide to Illuminated Manuscripts**. This work explains in detail how books were made and illuminated during the Middle Ages. *See* FINE ARTS.

Wisniewski, David. **Rain Player**. New York: Clarion Books, 1991. 32p. $15.95. ISBN 0-395-55112-9.

    The Mayan civilization was well organized and highly developed from A.D. 300 to A.D. 900 and in this original Mayan story, David Wisniewski takes the elements that were especially important to the culture and weaves a wonderful story, showing the importance of rain and other things in nature. Chac, the rain god, is highly revered, but a cocky young man, Pik, offends him and a drought is threatened. Pik bargains with Chac, and they agree to play the famous ball game *pok-a-tok*. If Pik wins, a drought will be avoided, but if he loses, a drought will occur, bringing certain death to the people. Chac allows Pik to assemble a team, so Pik requests help from the most powerful sources in Mayan society: the jaguar for strength, the quetzal for speed, and the cenote for deep wisdom. The game is played, and Pik wins with the help of his "team." The drought is avoided. The story combines many of the important elements of Mayan society into an entertaining and beautiful yet informative tale. The author includes a page of notes at the end of the book, giving the history of the Mayans and an explanation of how this work evolved and how the paper cuts were constructed.

————. **The Warrior and the Wise Man**. New York: Lothrop, Lee & Shepard, 1989. 32p. $16.00. ISBN 0-688-07889-3 (trade), 0-688-07890-7 (lib. bdg.).

    The age-old struggle between strength and wisdom are presented in this twelfth-century Japanese story featuring the twin sons of the emperor, Tozaemon and Toemon. Tozaemon is brave and fierce, a great warrior; Toemon is thoughtful and gentle, a wise man. The emperor needs to choose one of them to succeed him, so he puts them to a test. Whichever son can come back to him with a sample of each of the five eternal elements—the earth that is ever bountiful, the water that constantly quenches, the fire that burns forever, the wind that always blows, and the cloud that eternally covers—will become the new emperor. Tozaemon, being a brave warrior, heads out first and always gets his sample but creates massive destruction and damage along the way. Toemon, being thoughtful and wise, follows his brother and repairs the destruction. Tozaemon returns to the emperor first with all five samples, but the armies from each of the elements also arrive, wanting to kill him. Toemon again uses his wisdom to fight back the armies. Even though he doesn't succeed in bringing all five samples with him, Toemon is given the throne because strength is important, but it must be used in the service of wisdom. Author David Wisniewski explains how the paper cuts were made and how he gathered information for the story and illustrations in the author's notes on the last page.

Woods, Geraldine. **Science in Ancient Egypt**. This work describes the scientific discoveries and advancements in ancient Egypt. *See* SCIENCE.

Yep, Laurence. **The City of Dragons**. Illus. Jean Tseng and Mou-sien Tseng. This ancient Chinese folktale is told with the help of excellent artwork. *See* MYTHS, FOLKTALES, AND LEGENDS.

————. **The Khan's Daughter: A Mongolian Folktale**. Illus. Jean Tseng and Mou-sien Tseng. This folktale from Mongolia follows a sheepherder's son as he attempts to marry the khan's daughter. *See* MYTHS, FOLKTALES, AND LEGENDS.

Zeman, Ludmila. **Gilgamesh the King**. This is the first of three books portraying ancient Mesopotamia. *See* MYTHS, FOLKTALES, AND LEGENDS.

————. **The Last Quest of Gilgamesh**. This third book in the series retells the ancient tale from Mesopotamia. *See* MYTHS, FOLKTALES, AND LEGENDS.

————. **The Revenge of Ishtar**. This is the second book in the series that retells the ancient tale from Mesopotamia. *See* MYTHS, FOLKTALES, AND LEGENDS.

Chapter 15

SPORTS AND GAMES

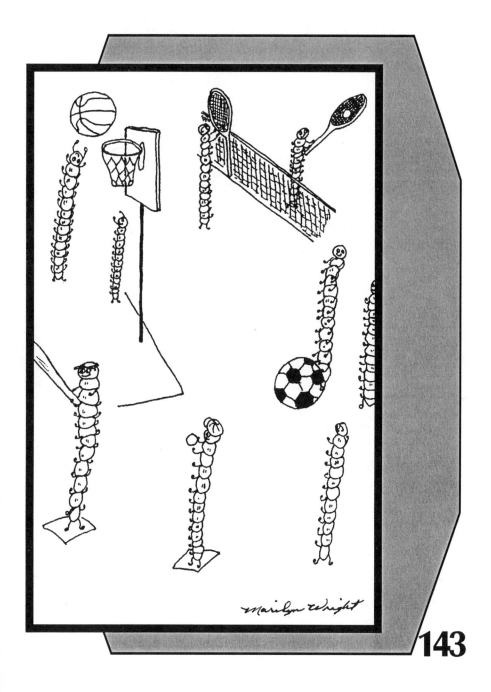

Students who love sports often enjoy reading fiction and nonfiction works involving sports and games. Titles included in this section are books teachers can share with students as read alouds, such as poetry selections, as well as books that students will enjoy on their own for pleasure reading or for information.

Bradley, Steve. **The Sure Thing**. A jockey refuses to throw the race and rides her horse to victory. This is part of a low level, high interest series of sports stories written in an upbeat, fast-paced manner. *See* HIGH INTEREST—LOW READING LEVEL.

Climo, Shirley. **Atalanta's Race: A Greek Myth**. A retelling of the ancient Greek myth emphasizes the importance of physical fitness. *See* MYTHS, FOLKTALES, AND LEGENDS.

Crutcher, Chris. **Ironman**. New York: Greenwillow, 1995. 181p. $14.00. ISBN 0-688-13503-X, 0-44-21971-X pa.
        As a football player, Bo Brewster is gifted, but unfortunately his temper and quick mouth get him kicked off the team. He finds himself enrolled in an anger-management class taught by a Japanese-American Texan, Mr. Nakatani. "Nak's Pack" meets early in the morning, before regular classes, consists of students with severe problems, and is the last step before expulsion. Nak, through patience and tough love, allows students to discover what their problems are and gives them tools to solve those problems. Through a long, hard process, Bo develops an understanding of himself that is aided by his sports talent and competitive nature. A myriad of the world's ills is discussed, and tied in with sports and the challenges they present. Much of the story is told through letters Bo writes—often in his head—to Larry King, the talk-show host.

————. **Stotan!** New York: Greenwillow, 1986. 183p. $14.00. ISBN 0-688-05715-2, 0-440-20080-6pa.
        Swimming is not a big sport in Great Falls, Montana, but Robert Frost High School does have an outdoor pool, a coach, Max, and a small team made up primarily of four senior students: Walker, Nortie, Lion, and Jeff. The coach devises Stotan Week, days of extremely difficult practices and workouts in the bitter cold: The idea is to test the participants' endurance. The four boys live together during that week, making swimming their top priority. However, much more than swimming

takes place as the boys get to know one another only to discover that each has major, deep-seated problems that need to be faced. Crutcher is a master at using sports as a vehicle for self-discovery, and he presents social problems in an up-front manner.

Hopkins, Lee Bennett, ed. **Extra Innings: Baseball Poems**. New York: Harcourt Brace Jovanovich, 1993. 40p. $14.95. ISBN 0-15-226833-2.
Hopkins has compiled 19 entertaining poems all having baseball as their theme. Each one deals with a different aspect of the game, ranging from "At Little League," by Patricia Hubbell, to a tribute to Joe DiMaggio in "Mighty Joe," by Lee Bennett Hopkins, to the famous "Casey at the Bat," by Ernest Lawrence Thayer. All the entries lend themselves to being read aloud, which makes them appropriate and fun to share with a baseball team or a physical-education class enjoying a baseball unit.

———. **Opening Days: Sports Poems**. Illus. Scott Medlock. New York: Harcourt Brace & Company, 1996. 37p. $16.00. ISBN 0-15-200270-7.
A poem about every popular sport is included in this collection. Sports fans can have fun with poems about karate, track and field, weight lifting, running, bicycling, swimming, basketball, football, ice skating, skiing, soccer, and tennis. A full-page color illustration accompanies each poem, making this a delightful book.

Krull, Kathleen. **Lives of the Athletes: Thrills, Spills (and What the Neighbors Thought)**. Illus. Kathryn Hewitt. New York: Harcourt Brace & Company, 1997. 95p. $19.00. ISBN 0-15-200806-3.
The lives of 20 world-famous athletes are described and celebrated in short chapters that include a biographical description and a full-page, color, cartoon-like illustration. Interesting and often humorous facts help make the athlete seem real, and a section at the end of each biography entitled "Athleticisms" gives additional tidbits of personal information. The athletes included are Jim Thorpe, Duke Kahanamoku, Babe Ruth, Red Grange, Johnny Weissmuller, Gertrude Ederle, Babe Didrikson Zaharias, Sonja Henie, Jesse Owens, Jackie Robinson, Sir Edmund Hillary, Maurice Connolly, Roberto Clemente, Wilma Rudolph, Arthur Ashe, Pete Maravich, Bruce Lee, Pelé, and Flo Hyman. An extensive bibliography is included.

Lankford, Mary D. **Hopscotch Around the World**. New York: Morrow Junior Books, 1992. 47p. $15.00. ISBN 0-688-08420-6.
Children around the world are more alike than different, as shown by the way hopscotch is played in various countries. The game's name might be different and have slightly different rules, but the similarities are amazing. Each two-page spread gives the country's name, location, a description of that country's version of the game, and the exact rules. Vivid illustrations help to tell the story.

————. **Jacks Around the World**. New York: Morrow Books, 1996. 40p. $16.00. ISBN 0-688-13707-5 (trade), 0-688-13708-3 (lib. bdg.).

    The rules may differ slightly and the game pieces might be bone, seeds, or small rocks rather than pronged metal or plastic pieces, but the game is the same—jacks. A great deal of research was done to determine that jacks is not only a common game around the world at this time, but it was also played in ancient Rome, China, and Greece. The basic universal rules are given, followed by a write-up and an illustration showing how the game is played in Brazil, Israel, Japan, New Zealand, China, Singapore, Somalia, South Korea, Thailand, Tibet, Trinidad and Tobago, Hawaii, Texas, and Zimbabwe. A bibliography and an index are included, along with some unanswered questions. Again we are struck with cultural sameness rather than difference.

Myers, Walter Dean. **Slam!** New York: Scholastic, 1996. 266p. $15.95. ISBN 0-590-48667-5.

    Slam, a Black kid living in the inner city, is at his best when he's on the basketball court. He's a gifted basketball player, but he is having to prove himself at a new school and is having a tough time academically. The result is giving him a bad attitude that influences his effectiveness on the court. Two main themes are presented in this book: life in the inner city and basketball. Slam's family is intact, but his father has problems keeping a job, which then causes him to drink too heavily, and his mother, who gives him encouragement and guidance, is involved with her sick mother. Slam's best friend, Ice, another excellent basketball player, is beginning to get into drugs, and Slam feels he needs to approach him and try to turn him around. Excellent descriptions of inner-city life are presented, and the basketball action is fast paced and well described. Anyone interested in basketball will be drawn into the descriptions and dynamics of the plays and players. Slam is a great player and has dreams of playing for the NBA, but the coach isn't letting Slam start until he is willing to be a team player and clean up his bad attitude. Therefore, scouts don't know about him, and he's becoming increasingly frustrated. As the story develops and all the subplots begin to merge, Slam does become a team player, he's allowed to be a starter, and his relationships with Ice, his girlfriend Mtisha, his teachers, and his family members improve. The book is a real page-turner for students hooked on basketball.

Thayer, Ernest Lawrence. **Casey at the Bat: A Ballad of the Republic, Sung in the Year 1988**. Illus. Patricia Polacco. New York: G. P. Putnam's Sons, 1988. 32p. $14.95. ISBN 0-399-21585-9, 0-399-21884-Xpa.

    The main part of this version of Casey is the retelling of the favorite baseball poem about the mighty Casey and his downfall, but this rendition adds a new twist. Casey is a cocky, overconfident Little League baseball star who feels he's above all the rules that apply to the other players. He feels he doesn't need to arrive on time because they couldn't possibly begin without him, the "star." By coming late, he attracts the negative attention of the "meanest, leanest, keenest ump in the Little

League," Harry Donovan. They go on to play the fateful game, and at the end the ump says he's sorry, but he "calls 'em the way he sees 'em." The father and son then walk home together, wondering what's for dinner. This humorous ending and Patricia Polacco's illustrations make the poem fun and alive.

Chapter 16
UNIQUE PRESENTATIONS

Marilyn Wright

Some works tell their story in such a unique and creative manner that they need to be highlighted and celebrated as special works. The uniqueness often helps to make the subject matter come alive, therefore helping the reader better understand what is presented.

Avi. **The Fighting Ground**. New York: J. B. Lippincott, 1984. 158p. $10.95. ISBN 0-397-32073-6 (trade), 0-397-32074-4 (lib. bdg.), 0-06-440185-5pa.

Twenty-four hours of the Revolutionary War are recounted in this unusual book, which is not formatted in chapters but by hours and minutes. For example, it begins on April 3, 1778, at 9:58. The next section is 10:15, then 10:25. Jonathan's older brother is a soldier, and his father is back from the war. He desperately wants to join the troops, but his father, who is disabled because of the war, refuses to let him go. Jonathan, age 13, glamorizes war and fantasizes about how exciting and wonderful it would be to be a part of the revolutionary forces. When Jonathan hears the local church bell tolling, meaning the army urgently needs troops, he runs off, without provisions or a gun. He joins the Corporal and heads off to war with no skills or training but with high enthusiasm. He ends up seeing that it isn't only the soldiers who are injured or killed but sometimes innocent families. He is captured by some Hessians fighting for the British and during the next 24 hours experiences the true horrors and injustices of war. He learns there aren't really good guys and bad guys but simply other human beings just like him fighting for a cause. The action is fast paced and written from the viewpoint of a boy who has a lot to learn. The short chapters move the story quickly and effectively. It's very appropriate for reluctant readers and is a terrific source when studying the Revolutionary War.

———. **Nothing but the Truth**. New York: Orchard, 1991. 177p. $15.00. ISBN 0-531-05959-6 (trade), 0-531-08559-7 (lib. bdg.), 0-380-71907-Xpa.

Phillip Malloy likes to hum along when the national anthem is played during homeroom at his school. This is fine, until he changes to Miss Narwin's homeroom. She feels this is disruptive behavior and sends him to the office. After his third referral, Phillip is suspended from school. His neighbor, a reporter, questions why he is home from school. When Phillip tells him, the reporter decides there's a story and puts it on the international news wires that a student was suspended from school for being patriotic. The reaction is far-reaching and beyond expectations, testing democracy and free speech. The entire book is told using diary entries, telephone conversations, news articles, speeches, memos, telegrams, letters, and conversations. It's a fascinating story using an unusual but highly effective style.

―――. **"Who Was That Masked Man, Anyway?"** New York: Orchard, 1992. 170p. $14.95. ISBN 0-531-05457-8 (trade), 0-531-08607-0 (lib. bdg.).

We often blame television for the poor performance of students academically and physically, but it's interesting to note the same ideas came up when radio first appeared. Parents were afraid schoolwork would suffer and children would become too "soft" if they spent too much time listening to the radio. Frankie Wattleson and his friend Mario Calvino are hooked on their favorite radio programs in 1945 and will do anything to listen to them. Frankie doesn't have a radio, so he goes to extreme measures to sneak into Mario's house next door to listen to their favorite programs. They live out the lives of their heroes—the Green Hornet, the Lone Ranger, and Buck Rodgers—by imagining they're solving the world's problems by doing what their superheroes would do. Actual excerpts from old radio programs are included. Frankie's older brother, Tom, wounded and suffering from shell shock, has just returned from fighting in World War II, which adds another dimension to the tale. The story gives an excellent window on life in the 1940s in the United States. The book is written entirely in dialogue because someone once bet Avi he couldn't write a book that way. This is an excellent example to use when studying writing conversation.

Bateson-Hill, Margaret. **Lao Lao of Dragon Mountain**. Chinese text Manyee Wan, illus. Francesca Pelizzoli, paper cuts Sha-Liu Qu. An ancient Chinese folktale is told using paper cuts. *See* FINE ARTS.

Blos, Joan W. **A Gathering of Days: A New England Girl's Journal, 1830–32**. New York: Charles Scribner's Sons, 1979. 144p. $12.00. ISBN 0-684-16340-3.

When Catherine Hall is 13, she begins keeping a diary of her life on a small farm in New Hampshire in 1830. Her mother has died, and she is in charge of the household and taking care of her little sister. Most diary entries are short, but they portray life as it was at that time and also tell the story of Catherine's life. She talks about the work on the farm, school, her family and her friends, the neighbors, the weather, illness, a runaway slave, holidays, her father's remarriage, a new stepbrother, and the death of her best friend, Cassie. She stops writing when she moves to live with her Aunt Lucy. There she can continue her studies and help her aunt with a new baby. The diary is given to Catherine's great-granddaughter, also named Catherine, in 1899. The story is fictitious but based on historical fact. It won the Newbery Award in 1980.

Crutcher, Chris. **Ironman**. A troubled student is helped through sports. The story is told through letters. *See* SPORTS AND GAMES.

Cushman, Karen. **Catherine, Called Birdy**. New York: Clarion Books, 1994. 169p. $13.95. ISBN 0-395-68186-3, 0-06-440584-2pa.
>Everyday life in a medieval English manor in 1290 is told through Catherine, better known as Birdy, a spunky 14-year-old. Mother has tried her best to teach her how to be a lady of the manor and to prepare her to be a good wife, but Catherine has resisted all the way. She would rather be outdoors roaming through the fields and exploring nature or taking care of her birds in the aviary, which is why she is call Birdy. Father wants to marry her off to someone of wealth so that he can gain wealth and status, but Catherine really doesn't want to be married to anyone yet. Medieval life is described as visitors come and go from the manor, especially suitors. Father finally decides she must marry an old man she nicknames Shaggy Beard, but the thought of marrying him is so distasteful that Birdy finds every way possible to get out of the deal. She runs away to her aunt, a two-day journey, but the aunt doesn't come up with any good ideas. So Birdy humbly goes back home prepared to bite the bullet and marry Shaggy Beard. To her surprise she learns that Shaggy Beard died in a brawl, and she is now promised to his son, Stephen, whom she understands is young, clean, and loves learning. She can live with that. The descriptions of manor life are detailed and graphic. All aspects of life are presented, including clothing, food, furniture, hygiene habits, farming methods, disease, and schooling. The entire story is told using diary entries. Each entry begins with a quote in italics celebrating a particular saint. This outstanding book earned the Newbery Award in 1994.

Kidd, Diana. **Onion Tears**. Illus. Lucy Montgomery. Nam-Huong, a Vietnamese refugee who has been so traumatized she no longer speaks, presents her story about everyday life in the regular text, but her deep, inner thoughts are written in italics to animals friends she had in Vietnam. *See* MULTICULTURAL.

Langley, Andrew, and Philip De Souza. **The Roman News**. Cambridge, MA: Candlewick Press, 1996. 32p. $16.00. ISBN 0-7636-0055-5.
>Imagine the Romans from 800 B.C.–A.D. 400 had newspapers. Imagine the newspaper contained the sections of our modern-day newspapers, including the main headlines plus feature articles reporting on everyday life, such as sports, business, politics, life at the time in the army, the city and the country, religion, women's interests, building, fashion, food, children's pages, and advertisements. The authors have used the newspaper format to present information about Roman civilization, dividing it into sections made to look like newspaper articles. This oversize book is jam-packed with information arranged in an intriguing manner sure to catch the reader's eye. The color illustrations, maps, decorative borders, sketches, and drawings help to explain the

articles in an informative and entertaining manner. The index and the time line make this a useful tool for research, but because of the unique format, it's fascinating to pore over for pleasure.

Müller, Claudia. **The Timeline of World Costume: From Fig Leaf to Street Fashion**. London: Thames and Hudson, 1992. Unpaged. $14.00. ISBN 0-500-01588-0.
   This impressive, oversize book shows the types of clothing worn by various peoples from around the world from 3000 B.C. through the twentieth century. The introduction points out many interesting facts about clothing throughout the ages and explains how to use the book. Each two-page spread includes clothing for a particular time period, arranged in three horizontal columns by geographical areas of the world. Each picture modeling clothing is assigned a number, which corresponds to a small explanation given on the bottom of the page. The amount of information packed into this book is outstanding, but what makes this book even more useful and interesting is that it is not a bound book. The large pages are folded over one another, allowing the pages to be stretched out fully, making this one huge timeline of clothing and costumes. The paper is heavy, so it stands up under use. This reference book can be used when studying any time period since 3000 B.C.

Nichol, Barbara. **Beethoven Lives Upstairs**. Illus. Scott Cameron. New York: Orchard, 1994. 48p. $14.00. ISBN 0-531-06828-5, 0-590-50830-Xpa.
   Ludwig van Beethoven's life is revealed one letter at a time through the letters written by Uncle Karl who lives in Salzburg, Germany, and his 10-year-old nephew, Christoph, who lives in Vienna, Beethoven's home city. Christoph is quite disturbed because a crazy man has rented a room in their house, and he wants his uncle to talk his mother into kicking the man out. Through the letters, we learn that the crazy man is Beethoven toward the end of his life after deafness has set in, and he's in the process of composing the Ninth Symphony. Beethoven's progress is followed as Christoph eventually makes friends with the ill-tempered, eccentric old man. Uncle Karl, a music student, researches Beethoven's life and sends that information back to Christoph, so a great deal is revealed about Beethoven as the letters continue. The illustrations are effective in showing the historical setting. This easy-to-read picture book does a wonderful job of celebrating the great composer's life.

Parker, Nancy Winslow. **Locks, Crocs, and Skeeters: The Story of the Panama Canal**. New York: Greenwillow, 1996. 32p. $16.00. ISBN 0-688-12241-8.
   The saga of the building of the Panama Canal is fascinating, but the manner in which it is presented in this book is unusual as well. James Stanley Gilbert worked in Panama during the building of the canal and wrote poetry about it. Part I of this book is his poem, "Beyond the Chagres," describing the enormous obstacles met while building, including

malaria, alligators, boa constrictors, scorpions and spiders, and a host of other dangers that made life nearly impossible. Cartoonlike drawings give the poem a light touch, but the seriousness of the situation is clearly described. Part II tells the story with descriptive text, maps and sketches, and short biographies of people important to the canal, including Vasco de Balboa, Ferdinand de Lesseps, Theodore Roosevelt, John Stevens, George Goethals, and William Gorgas. This multifaceted book fits well with many curriculums.

Peterson, Gail. **Greg Hildebrandt's Book of Three-Dimensional Dragons**. Illus. Greg Hildebrandt, design and paper engineering Keith Moseley. Boston: Little, Brown, 1994. Unpaged. $18.95. ISBN 0-316-15240-4.

Dragons are marvelous, legendary creatures that seem to appear in many cultures during many time periods. This large, colorful pop-up book includes five extraordinary dragons that pop out and wiggle when the page is turned, making them come alive. The dragons include the wyvern dragon, the Amphiptere, the Lindworm, a Chinese dragon, and the Dragon of St. George. The text accompanying each dragon explains the meaning of the legend and where and when it appeared in history and literature. This book is a visual feast loved by everyone.

Powell, Anton, and Philip Steele. **The Greek News**. Cambridge, MA: Candlewick Press, 1996. 32p. $16.00. ISBN 1-56402-874-7.

The Greeks from 800 B.C.–300 B.C. didn't have newspapers, but if they had, they might have looked similar to this book. Each page resembles a modern-day newspaper, with large, bold headings, maps, drawings, sketches, color pictures and cartoons, and an informative article. The major headlines of the day are addressed, along with "lifestyle" sections that deal with politics, army and navy life, trade, sports, women's concerns, school life, theater, building, housing, health, food, farming, fashion, and there are special reports on the gods, Spartan life, and the philosophers. An index and a time line are included. Each page in this oversize book is colorful and informative, making it useful for perusing for pleasure as well as an outstanding resource for research when studying ancient Greece.

Ruby, Lois. **Steal Away Home**. New York: Macmillan, Maxwell Macmillan International, 1994. 192p. $16.00. ISBN 0-02777883-5.

This unique time-travel work is set in modern-day Lawrence, Kansas, and then flips back to the same location in a pre-Civil War setting, 1856. Present-day Dana isn't very excited about remodeling the old house her parents are hoping to turn into a bed and breakfast until a skeleton is found in a hidden room. The reader is then led back and forth between the two time periods to discover that the house involved runaway slaves and the Underground Railroad. A great deal of history is revealed as the reader learns about the mystery involving the skeleton.

Smythe, Reginald Oliver. **Safari: My Trip to Africa**. San Anselmo, CA: Traveling Bear Press, 1995. Unpaged. $25.00. ISBN 0-9643771-0-1.

Reginald Oliver Smythe is actually a teddy bear that took a trip to Africa, along with his owner, Susan Hoy. Susan returns from the safari eager to tell her story and chooses to do so through the eyes of a bear stuck into a backpack. The book is actually a diary of the month-long trip, recorded on heavy, mottled paper, handwritten, and spiral bound. It ties shut with a heavy, braided string. The text is Susan's daily entries, told by Reginald. It's informative yet light and cute, and each page is filled with colorful sketches of things encountered at the time of the entry. The landscape, birds, flowers, trees, animals large and small, and even the night sky of Africa are beautifully sketched, filling the book with valuable information. The book's maps help in making sense of the story. Many additional touches are added, including the travel itinerary, tickets, and even postcards sent to friends. This is a clever and fun way to learn about Africa.

Talbott, Hudson, and Mark Greenberg. **Amazon Diary: The Jungle Adventures of Alex Winters**. New York: G. P. Putnam's Sons, 1996. 49p. $15.95. ISBN 0-399-22916-7.

Alex Winters' adventure to the Amazon jungle begins with the small Cessna crashing, injuring Alex and the pilot, Mike, and leaving them stranded in the middle of the Amazon forest. A tribe of Amazonian Indians, the Yanomamis, take Alex and Mike to their home, where they recuperate and then enjoy adventures in the wilds of the Amazon rain forest. The entire adventure is told in diary form, with many actual photographs of the Yanomamis and their part of the world. Vivid drawings and sketches of the wildlife and plant life fill each page. The authors actually traveled to this part of the world and became enthralled with the stone-age tribe, still living in harmony with nature. An address is included if the reader wants to learn more about the Yanomamis and their current situation.

Williams, Marcia, retold and illus. **The Iliad and the Odyssey**. Cambridge, MA: Candlewick Press, 1996. 35p. $17.99. ISBN 0-7636-0053-9.

Understanding the story of *The Iliad* and *The Odyssey* can be difficult for students, but Marcia Williams gives the reader an excellent tool to make the job easier. She presents the story in cartoon form, with text written beneath each picture giving the story line. Each cartoon box has colorful drawings along with the conversations and thoughts of the characters—usually funny or silly. Chapter headings are in large print at the top of each page, along with colorful borders depicting symbols that further illustrate the action. The reader may flip through the book, quickly getting the main flow of the story, or may take a great deal of time to carefully read and examine each picture, symbol, drawing, and funny comment. What a fun way to present a difficult subject!

LITERATURE LINKS

Many of the titles listed in this book can be used in multiple curricular areas. The following chart tells in which chapters each title will be found. An "A" denotes which chapter contains the main annotation and an "X" shows which chapters contain a brief entry.

TITLES	Biographies (BI)	English–Classics (ENG-CL)	English–Use of Language (ENG-USE)	Fine Arts (FI)	Greatest of the Latest (GR)	High Interest–Low Reading Level (HI)	Mathematics (MA)	Multicultural (MU)	Myths, Folktales, and Legends (MFL)	Poetry (PO)	Read Alouds (RA)	Science (SC)	Social Studies–U.S. History (SS-HI)	Soc. Studies–Ancient/Early Cultures (SS-A/E)	Sports and Games (SG)	Unique Presentations (UP)
Adventures of Tom Sawyer, The					A											
Advice for a Frog										X		A				
After the Dancing Days												A				
Against the Storm								A								
Ali, Child of the Desert														A		
Amazon Diary														X		A
And One for All													A			
And the Green Grass Grew All Around									X	A						
Angela Weaves a Dream				A				X						X		
Angles							A									
Anna to the Infinite Power												A				
Anno's Hat Tricks							A									
Anno's Magic Seeds							A									
Anno's Math Games II							A									
Anno's Math Games III							A									

A=Annotated Entry; X=Cross-Reference

TITLES	(BI)	(ENG-CL)	(ENG-USE)	(FI)	(GR)	(HI)	(MA)	(MU)	(MFL)	(PO)	(RA)	(SC)	(SS-HI)	(SS-A/E)	(SG)	(UP)
Anno's Mysterious Multiplying Jar							A									
Apprenticeship of Lucas Whitaker, The					X							A	X			
Area and Volume							A									
Arithmetic							A		X							
Atalanta's Race: A Greek Myth								A						X	X	
Ballad of Lucy Whipple, The					A							X				
Ballot Box Battle, The	A											X				
Barn, The					A											
Bartholomew Fair														A		
Bearstone		A										X				
Beduins' Gazelle														A		
Beethoven Lives Upstairs	X		X													A
Best Children's Books in the World, The			X					A								
Beyond the Western Sea: Book One					X								A			
Beyond the Western Sea: Book Two					X								A			
Bibles and Bestiaries			A										X			
Bobbin Girl, The													A			
Bone from a Dry Sea, A													A			
Boy of the Painted Cave													A			
Brian's Winter											X	A				
Bridge to Terabithia		A										X				
Brown Angels								X	A							
Buffalo Gals													A			
Cache of Jewels and Other Collective Nouns, A			A													
California Blue													A			
Candy Man, The						A										
Casey at the Bat									X						A	
Cat Running													A			
Catherine, Called Birdy														X		A
Cay, The		A														

TITLES	(BI)	(ENG-CL)	(ENG-USE)	(FI)	(GR)	(HI)	(MA)	(MU)	(MFL)	(PO)	(RA)	(SC)	(SS-HI)	(SS-A/E)	(SG)	(UP)
Celebrate America: In Poetry and Art				A						X			X			
Celebrating Women in Mathematics and Science	X						A					X				
Children of the Yucatan								A								
Chinese Siamese Cat, The								A								
Chocolate Moose for Dinner, A			A													
Circles							A									
City of Dragons, The									A					X		
City of Gold and Lead, The		X									A					
Classic Poems to Read Aloud										A	X					
Cool Salsa								A	X							
Counting on Frank							A									
Crossing, The								A								
Dandelions												A				
Danger on Midnight River						A										
Dangerous Skies				A												
Dar and the Spear-Thrower														A		
Dark Is Rising, The		A														
Dark Stairs, The											A					
Dark Thirty, The								A			X					
Dead Letter											A					
Demi's Secret Garden										A		X				
Dia's Story Cloth				X				A								
Discovering the Iceman														A		
Downriver												A				
Dragon Kite of the Autumn Moon				X										A		
Dragons Are Singing Tonight, The										A	X					
Dragon's Gate								X				A				
Dragon's Tale and Other Animal Fables of the Chinese Zodiac, The									A					X		
Dwarf Giant, The				A										X		
Egypt Game, The		A												X		
18th Emergency, The						A										
Escape from Fire Mountain						A										

TITLES	(BI)	(ENG-CL)	(ENG-USE)	(FI)	(GR)	(HI)	(MA)	(MU)	(MFL)	(PO)	(RA)	(SC)	(SS-HI)	(SS-A/E)	(SG)	(UP)
Extra Innings: Baseball Poems										X				A		
Falling Up					X					A						
Far North					X						X	A				
Fighting Ground, The						X							X			A
For Home and Country												A				
Fortune									A					X		
Forty-Third War, The								A								
Game for Fools, A						A										
Gathering of Days, A													X			A
Gathering of Pearls					X			A								
Gathering the Sun				X				A	X							
Ghana, Mali, Songhay														A		
Ghost Canoe					A							X	X			
Gilgamesh the King									A					X		
Giver, The		A								X						
Go Hang a Salami! I'm a Lasagna Hog!			A													
Going Home								A								
Golden Tales									A		X			X		
Good Night, Mr. Tom		A														
Good Queen Bess	A													X		
Gorgon Slayer, The							A									
Grandfather Tang's Story: A Tale Told with Tangrams							A		X							
Grass Sandals: The Travels of Basho	X									A				X		
Grass Songs										A			X			
Great Brain Is Back, The					A					X						
Greek News, The														X		A
Greg Hildebrandt's Book of Three-Dimensional Dragons				X										X		A
Gypsy Game, The					A											
Harriet Beecher Stowe and the Beecher Preachers	A												X			
Harris and Me						X					A					
Hatchet		X				X					X	A				

TITLES	(BI)	(ENG-CL)	(ENG-USE)	(FI)	(GR)	(HI)	(MA)	(MU)	(MFL)	(PO)	(RA)	(SC)	(SS-HI)	(SS-A/E)	(SG)	(UP)
Her Stories								X	A		X					
History of the United States Through Art, A			A										X			
Hopscotch Around the World								X							A	
House on Mango Street, The								A								
How Much Is a Million?							A									
Hundred Penny Box, The						A		X								
I Think I Thought, and Other Tricky Verbs			A													
If I Were in Charge of the World and Other Worries										A						
If You Made a Million							A									
Iliad and the Odyssey, The								X						X		A
In a Pickle, and Other Funny Idioms			A													
Irish Cinderlad, The									A							
Ironman															A	X
It's Perfectly Normal												A				
Jabberwocky		A								X	X					
Jacks Around the World								X							A	
Jacob Have I Loved		A														
Jaguar in the Rain Forest												A				
Jip: His Story				A									X			
John Brown: One Man Against Slavery	A												X			
Jouanah: A Hmong Cinderella								X	A							
Julie of the Wolves		X										A				
June 29, 1999												A				
Juniper		A												X		
Keepers										A						
Khan's Daughter: A Mongolian Folktale, The									A					X		
King Who Rained, The			A													
King's Chessboard, The							A							X		
Kites Sail High: A Book About Verbs			A													

TITLES	(BI)	(ENG-CL)	(ENG-USE)	(FI)	(GR)	(HI)	(MA)	(MU)	(MFL)	(PO)	(RA)	(SC)	(SS-HI)	(SS-A/E)	(SG)	(UP)
Knight's Handbook, The			A											X		
Lao Lao of Dragon Mountain			A					X	X					X		X
Last Quest of Gilgamesh, The									A					X		
Latino Rainbow: Poems About Latino Americans	X							A		X						
Legend of Red Horse Cavern, The					A											
Leonardo Da Vinci	A		X													
Librarian Who Measured the Earth, The	X						A					X		X		
Library Card, The				A												
Life Doesn't Frighten Me			X							A						
Lion's Paw, The											A					
Little Pigeon Toad, A		A														
Lives of the Artists	X		A													
Lives of the Athletes	X														A	
Lives of the Musicians	X		A													
Lives of the Writers	A															
Locks, Crocs, & Skeeters	X										X		X			A
Log Cabin Quilt, The												X	A			
Long Silk Strand, The									X					A		
Love Letters										A						
Lyddie													A			
Mad As a Wet Hen! And Other Funny Idioms			A													
Maestro, The				A												
Magic Tapestry, The									A					X		
Man Who Counted, The							A							X		
Many Luscious Lollipops: A Book About Adjectives			A													
Maples in the Mist										A				X		
Market!							A									
Martin Luther King	A						X						X			
Marvelous Math							A			X						
Math Curse							A									

TITLES	(BI)	(ENG-CL)	(ENG-USE)	(FI)	(GR)	(HI)	(MA)	(MU)	(MFL)	(PO)	(RA)	(SC)	(SS-HI)	(SS-A/E)	(SG)	(UP)
Mathematicians Are People, Too	X						A				X					
Merry-Go-Round: A Book About Nouns		A														
Metropolis				X										A		
Midwife's Apprentice, The														A		
Minty: A Story of Young Harriet Tubman	A												X			
Miro in the Kingdom of the Sun									A					X		
Missing May		A														
Mississippi Mud										A			X			
Moon Lady, The														A		
More Sideways Arithmetic from Wayside School							A									
Mr. Was					A											
Mrs. Frisby and the Rats of NIMH	A										X					
My Brother Sam Is Dead	X												X			
My First Music Book			A								X					
My Side of the Mountain	X										X	A				
Mythical Birds & Beasts from Many Lands								X	A		X			X		
Nightjohn						X							A			
Nothing but the Truth																A
Number Patterns							A									
Numbers							A									
On My Honor						A					X					
On the Far Side of the Mountain											X	A				
One Grain of Rice: A Mathematical Folktale				X			A							X		
Onion Tears							A									X
Opening Days: Sports Poems										X					A	
Parrot in the Oven: Mi Vida/A Novel								A			X					
Pass It On								X	A							
Pink and Say													A			
Plots and Players														A		
Pool of Fire, The		X									A					

TITLES	(BI)	(ENG-CL)	(ENG-USE)	(FI)	(GR)	(HI)	(MA)	(MU)	(MFL)	(PO)	(RA)	(SC)	(SS-HI)	(SS-A/E)	(SG)	(UP)
Prairie Songs													A			
Project: A Perfect World					A											
Quadrilaterals						A										
Quetzal, Sacred Bird of the Cloud Forest									X			X		A		
Rain Player									X					A		
Random House Book of Poetry for Children, The										A	X					
Rascal												X	A			
Red Heels, The									A				X			
Red Pony, The		A									X					
Revenge of Ishtar, The									A					X		
Rock Jockeys, The					A											
Roll of Thunder, Hear My Cry	X							X					A			
Roman News, The														X		A
Roman Numerals I to MM							A									
Sacred River														A		
Safari—My Trip to Africa																A
Sarah, Plain and Tall					A								X			
Save Queen of Sheba													X			
Savitri: A Tale of Ancient India									A							
Science in Ancient China												A		X		
Science in Ancient Egypt												A		X		
Science in Ancient Greece												A		X		
Science in Ancient Mesopotamia												A		X		
Science in Early Islamic Culture												A		X		
Secret Places										A						
Seventh Crystal, The					A											
Shabanu, Daughter of the Wind														A		
Shadow of the Dragon								A								
Shark in the Sea												A				
Shiloh											A					
Shiloh Season					A											

TITLES	(BI)	(ENG-CL)	(ENG-USE)	(FI)	(GR)	(HI)	(MA)	(MU)	(MFL)	(PO)	(RA)	(SC)	(SS-HI)	(SS-A/E)	(SG)	(UP)
Sierra										X		A				
Sign of the Beaver, The											X	A	X			
Sing Down the Moon												A				
Sing Me a Death Song						X					A					
Sir Gawain and the Loathly Lady									A					X		
Sitti and the Cats									A					X		
Sixteen Hand Horse, The			A													
Slam!				X											A	
Slave Dancer, The		X										A				
Socrates and the Three Little Pigs							A									
Someone Is Hiding on Alcatraz Island						A				X						
Song of the Gargoyle										X			A			
Sootface: An Ojibwa Cinderella Story									A				X			
Sparrow Hawk Red								X		A						
Spite Fences												A				
Starry Messenger	X											A				
Statistics						A										
Steal Away Home													X			A
Stone Fox					A											
Stotan!														A		
Streams to the River, River to the Sea											X	A				
Summer of the Swans, The		A														
Sunita Experiment, The								A								
Sure Thing, The						A								X		
Sweetwater Run, The	X											A				
Tarot Says Beware										A						
There's a Boy in the Girl's Bathroom										A						
They're Off!												A				
Third Planet, The											A					
Three Princes, The								X	A					X		
Timeline of World Costume, The														X		A
Timothy of the Cay		A														

TITLES	(BI)	(ENG-CL)	(ENG-USE)	(FI)	(GR)	(HI)	(MA)	(MU)	(MFL)	(PO)	(RA)	(SC)	(SS-HI)	(SS-A/E)	(SG)	(UP)
Topsy-Turvy Emperor of China, The														A		
Tortilla Factory, The							A									
Triangles						A										
True Confessions of Charlotte Doyle, The		A									X		X			
Twisted Summer											A					
Under the Mummy's Spell											X			A		
Underground Railroad, The													A			
Velvet Room, The		A														
View from Saturday, The					A						X					
Voices of Silence, The					A											
Walking the Bridge of Your Nose			A							X	X					
Warrior and the Wise Man, The				X					X					A		
Watcher, The					A											
Watsons Go to Birmingham—1963, The					X						X		A			
Wave of the Sea-Wolf, The									X				A			
Weasel						X					A		X			
Where the Red Fern Grows		X									A					
White Mountains, The		X									A					
"Who Was That Masked Man, Anyway?"			X										X			A
Wise Child		A												X		
Witch of Blackbird Pond, The		A											X			
Wolf Rider: A Tale of Terror						A					X					
Wrinkle in Time, A		A														
Yeh-Shen									A					X		

AUTHOR-TITLE INDEX